EMBRACED

EMBRACED

Experiencing God's Father Heart of Love

BOB CARROLL

Printed in Canada

Print ISBN: 978-1-4866-2328-0
eBook ISBN: 978-1-4866-2329-7

Word Alive Press
119 De Baets Street, Winnipeg, MB R2J 3R9
www.wordalivepress.ca

Cataloguing in Publication may be obtained through Library and Archives
Canada

This book is dedicated to Audrey, my wife of forty-three years. I want to thank you for being my friend and partner both in life and ministry. I would not be who I am today without your love, support, spiritual wisdom, and prayers. You are God's gift to me.

CONTENTS

ACKNOWLEDGEMENTS

There are so many people who deserve to be acknowledged for their contributions to this book. Here are a few whose input and help deserve special thanks.

I would first like to thank my wife Audrey for the countless hours of work she put into this book, editing, clarifying, formatting, offering helpful suggestions, and staying calm. I could not have done it without you. Thanks is not enough.

I would like to thank my children, their spouses, and my grandchildren for their love and encouragement throughout this project. My son Nathan was extremely helpful to me and invested many hours of editing, clarifying, and providing valuable feedback and suggestions. You have made this book better than I ever could. Thanks to my daughter Amanda for her cover photography and Shane for his design ideas. Thanks to my son Joel and grandson Sully for appearing on the cover.

My thanks to those of you who took the time to read through my draft and offer helpful insights and ideas, along with heaps of encouragement. Your investment of time is greatly appreciated.

I would also like to thank my church family at Harvest Vineyard Christian Fellowship for their prayers and words of encouragement during the writing of this book. You guys are amazing and we love you deeply! Thank you for loving us, opening your lives to us, and making us feel like we belong.

I would especially like to thank James for his boldness at the age of seventeen in sharing with me a word from God that I should write a book. Despite my cool response at first, I did listen to God and the proof is now in your hands.

Many thanks to the people at Word Alive Press, especially Jen, Ariana, and Evan, for all their support, encouragement, and helpful ideas. It's been a true joy working with you.

I would also like to thank the many, many people I have had the privilege of knowing, loving, and serving through more than forty years of pastoral ministry. My relationships with you have taught me a lifetime's worth about God's work in people's lives.

Thanks to those of you who have freely shared your personal stories in this book. Thanks for your honesty, courage, and vulnerability. I believe the Father will use your stories to impact many.

Lastly, but most importantly, I would like to thank my Heavenly Father, who found this lost, fearful, fatherless boy and chose to become my loving Father. You have been faithful to Your promise to be *"a father to the fatherless"* (Psalm 68:5). I feel such deep gratitude for the undeserved mercy, kindness, and love You have constantly shown me. The love I feel in my heart for You is sometimes too much to contain! You have embraced me as a Father throughout my entire life. I can hardly wait to be embraced by You for all eternity!

FOREWORD

Bob Carroll. Who is he and why does his book matter? The who and the why are intertwined in the what of Bob's story. Bob is a person who writes from out of his life, not from a desire to add fame or fortune to his life. What he writes is an expression of who he is. Bob is a person of authenticity, honesty, integrity, and humility. His life's journey into the Father's heart is a journey of experiencing life, and that abundantly. He invites us to experience that same journey.

Bob's thoughts and insights are mined from the depths of scriptural passages, theological insights, pastoral experiences, personal reflections, and other people's stories. Bob's teaching is firmly planted on the road of real life. He brings the truth of our heavenly Father's personhood down to earth in ways that allow each of us to connect with the Father in meaningful ways.

I have known Bob both personally and professionally for decades. He succeeded me in my pastoral role, he was my pastor for over a decade, and I joined his accountability group of ministry workers a few years ago. In each of these life intersections, Bob has been consistent in his commitment to be fully obedient to the Father, to holistically represent Jesus with all his mind, body, soul, and spirit, and to faithfully fellowship with the Holy Spirit, to regularly be filled with the Spirit, and to daily follow His leading.

In other words, Bob is the real deal. Just ask his wife and children. He lives what he preaches; he preaches what he lives. Just ask his congregations. He shares from the pulpit what he wrestles with every day. Bob knows how to have fun. Just ask him about his motorcycling experiences. Bob has a heart for the disadvantaged. Just ask the poor, the orphans, the widows, and the outsiders with whom he has come into contact. Bob does not enjoy confrontation. . . I can identify. But he is not afraid to speak the truth as Jesus directs with a love that issues from the heart of the Father.

Bob's book can change you as you intentionally pray the prayers at the end of each chapter, as you work through the exercises that he includes within the various chapters, and as you have ears to hear what the Spirit is saying to you... and then just do it!

Bob is a sure guide because he has trodden all the paths he will lead you along in this book. Those paths are well worn with his faithful and repetitive obedience, but they are not dusty paths—he has watered those well-trodden paths with his tears of repentance, release, and intercession. May you hear the gentle call of the Father and experience the embrace of His love as you walk with Bob through this book.

—Dr. Ralph J. Korner
Professor of Biblical Studies
Taylor Seminary of Kairos University

INTRODUCTION

I was born into a father wound waiting to happen. And happen it did.

The only childhood memory I have of my father is of him yelling at me. When I was four years old, my parents' separation necessitated that my mom, brothers, and I move to another house. My dad rented a truck to help us. As I loaded several of my plastic toy soldiers onto the truck, to make sure they got to our new house, he angrily yelled at me, "Get those **** soldiers out of here!" I was stricken with terror at this unexpected outburst and slinked away, thankful that he had been preoccupied by carrying a heavy piece of furniture and was unable to hit me. His anger and dismissal of me gave me a sense of rejection, a fear that left me wounded and insecure.

The story of the broken relationship with my father, who was a very broken man, has defined who I am at my core and how I relate to other people. This defining power has been a debilitating force in me throughout my life. I've spent years struggling with fear, low self-esteem, and insecurity. Yet by God's grace I have been drawn into an increasing experience of the Heavenly Father's love for me. As a result, I have received an amazing work of healing that redeemed the pain that has held so much power over me.

This book has been sixty-five years in the making. Through hurt and healing, pain and grace, God has fathered me, and along the way He has taught me how to be a father. In this process, the Heavenly Father has given me a message about His heart of love that has become my life message to share with others.

This book is about an encounter with God's love.

Knowing God's love is a gift He offers us all. Many people, whether they recognize it or not, have a deep longing for this love at the centre of their being. They long to be known and loved. They have a desire to be known and loved by God as their Father.

Sadly, scores of people have never encountered this kind of love. They have engaged with the idea of God's love on an intellectual level, but a relationship with Him cannot grow deeper from only an idea.

God the Father, the One who created and sustains all things, wants to give people an *experience* of His love that exceeds anything they have ever known. He offers people an encounter with His love that will impact their whole being—heart and mind—as well as their past, present, and future lives, even extending to bringing new life to other relationships.

This book is also an invitation.

An experience of the Father heart of God is available to each of us. We all can discover His love, which brings about incredible grace, joy, freedom, and healing in our lives and will spill over to be a blessing to others.

Perhaps deep down you have a sense that there is much more to the love of God than what you are currently experiencing. You have a genuine desire in your heart to feel the love of your Heavenly Father, who is passionate, tender, and kind. Perhaps you know how empty it can be to go through lifeless motions of prayer, Bible reading, worship, serving, etc. out of a dry sense of religious duty. You find yourself crying out like a child for someone to notice you, spend time with you, and tell you how important you are to them. You carry this longing to know in your heart how much delight the Father takes in you, and to see His smiling face looking upon you even now. You long to hear Him say that you matter to Him. You desire to feel safe and secure in the care of the One who will always protect, guide, and stay near to you. You desire a relationship with the Father that is heart-to-heart, not just head-to-head.

He gathers the lambs in his arms and carries them close to his heart.
—Isaiah 40:11

No matter what stage of life you're in, this desire never ends. Many learn to suppress this longing, explain it away, or give up hope of ever experiencing love like this. But try as they might, the desire persists.

God is reawakening this longing in His people so they might embark on a renewed pursuit of His heart of love. He wants to breathe new life into hearts that have become tired, defeated, cold, dry, and shut down, and He is inviting us to return to the Father-child relationship described in Romans:

The Spirit you received does not make you slaves, so that you live in fear again; rather, the Spirit you received brought about your adoption to sonship. And by him we cry, "Abba, Father." The Spirit himself testifies with our spirit that we are God's children.

—Romans 8:15–16

Over the years, I have discovered that encountering the Father heart of God and experiencing His love has the been the most life-transforming gift of grace I have ever received. My wife Audrey will tell you that when I'm living intimately connected to the Father's love, I am a better person, husband, father, and friend, with God's love extending to every facet of my life. She says I am at my best when I live out of my sonship as a deeply loved child of the Heavenly Father.

This love continues to change me from a head-knowledge type of a person to one who both understands and experiences God's loving presence more deeply. I am writing this book to chart a path for you to experience a transformation in your life as a deeply loved son or daughter of the Heavenly Father.

These pages have been birthed from my study of the scriptures, my own personal encounter with the Father's love, as well as the experience of journeying with many other people over the years. This book comes from the heart of God to my heart... and to yours.

God's love is real, life-changing, and restorative—beyond what anyone could ever imagine. It is the only true and lasting source of security, identity, and value. This love is ultimately discovered through the sacrificial death and resurrection of God's Son, Jesus Christ, who is the only source of true salvation from the sin and brokenness that blocks us from experiencing God's love and wholeness. Through Christ alone, we can experience abundant life on earth and eternal life in heaven, all with full access to the love of our Heavenly Father. This is what God wants you to experience.

Romans 5:5 says that *"God's love has been poured out into our hearts through the Holy Spirit."* As you read this book, I invite you to ask the Holy Spirit to give you a fresh revelation of the Father's love. All you need to bring to this journey is a childlike faith and an open and hungry heart—a heart that deeply longs for a genuine encounter with the Father. May what Philip asked of Jesus also be the desire of your heart: *"Lord, show us the Father and that will be enough for us"* (John 14:8).

Here is a prayer for you to pray as this journey begins:

Heavenly Father,
I long for You, for Your love. I long to know how much You love me. I need to experience Your tenderness, care, and closeness. I want to feel deeply loved by You. I need to know that I matter to You. May Your Holy Spirit pour out Your love into my heart. I want to know You as Your perfect Son Jesus knew You—in profound intimacy.

Thank You for Your great love for me. I want to experience Your love like never before. I bring to You an open, hungry heart. I give thanks that You are a good Father who gives good gifts to Your children—and that means me!
In Jesus's name, amen.

GROWING UP FATHERLESS

Chapter One

I am the youngest of four boys. My father was a Canadian soldier who met my mom, a Dutch teenager, in Holland at the end of World War II. The Canadian Armed Forces played a critical role in the liberation of Holland from Nazi occupation in 1945. In the midst of celebrating the end of the war, my mom became pregnant with my oldest brother. Shortly thereafter, my father was shipped back to Canada to be reunited with his then-current wife and young son, my half-brother.

Just over a year later my mother, now twenty-one years of age, packed up her life and baby and sailed to Canada, along with many other war brides, to rejoin and marry my father. Sadly, their marriage was doomed before it began. Before my mother arrived, my father's first marriage failed due to his lifestyle of alcoholism and unfaithfulness. These dynamics would tragically continue into his second marriage.

When my mother arrived in Canada, she and my father began their life together as husband and wife. As a young immigrant in a brand-new country, my mother lacked many of the skills necessary to manage and maintain a home in those post-war days. On top of that, her English was very poor, creating even more challenges, and she was often hurtfully teased by her new husband's family.

Despite these challenges, they lived together as husband and wife for about a dozen years and had three more boys together. During these tumultuous years, my father continued to engage in extramarital affairs, which he made no effort to conceal from my mother.

Along with this, his persistent drinking had an increasing impact on our home. At times his drunkenness made him behave kindly—he occasionally returned home from drinking bearing gifts and bringing food—but more often it manifested in anger, rage, and physical violence, particularly towards my mom and oldest brother. When he became a teen, my brother tried to stand up to my dad, which resulted in fistfights.

My mom had a memory of me as a toddler calling out from my bed at night for my father: "Daddy, Daddy!" But he never came, never attended to my cry. This was heart-breaking for my mom. She recalls that the pain she experienced, along with her deep desire to be the best parent she could be, led her to rekindle her relationship with God through prayer.

My father walked out on our family when I was four years old.

My mother found us a small house to rent. A Christian landlord owned the house and treated this single immigrant mother and her four boys with compassion and generosity.

The greatest legacy of our landlord's kindness came in the form of an invitation for us to join his family at their church. Every Sunday, his family of seven and ours of five packed into his station wagon. Thankfully there were no seatbelt laws in those days!

Eventually, through connecting with a church family, my mom and brothers all gave their lives to Jesus. My own decision to follow Christ came later.

My mom did a wonderful job raising us four boys alone, a mammoth task for any single parent. Our family was certainly dysfunctional, owing to the devastating effects of my dad's alcoholism and the breakdown of my parents' marriage. Despite the challenges, my mother did her best to love, care, and provide for us all, demonstrating sacrifice, resilience, and faith. These themes were highlighted at her funeral at the age of ninety as our family and friends gathered to honour and remember her.

My background is the root of many wounds I've had to identify and address over the years. At times I have struggled with insecurity, shame, fearfulness, and feeling unloved. I've often assumed that people would dislike me, compelling me to earn their love and positive attention. As a result, I tend to be a people-pleaser, driven by a fear of disappointing those around me (the *"fear of man"* described in Proverbs 29:25).

I also came to recognize an orphan spirit within me, a sense that I don't belong and am always looking for someone to love me, especially a father figure. Sometimes I find it hard to trust people. I've often believed the lie that no one will take care of me so I have to look out for myself.

Thankfully, God has brought me much healing over the years. I've discovered that healing for these deep emotional wounds is often a progressive and layered process. My journey continues even to this day.

Returning to the Memory

This journey of healing began in my thirties. During a time of prayer ministry, I was invited to revisit that painful memory of my father yelling at me when I was four years old as I placed my toy soldiers onto the moving truck. I remember feeling afresh the pain of my father's anger and rejection.

A Spirit-led person encouraged me to ask Jesus where He had been when this hurtful event happened. A vivid picture came to my mind of Jesus kneeling down right beside me, His arms around me in loving protection. With a compassionate look in His eyes, Jesus said to me, "Bobby, you don't deserve this. I'm here to protect you. I love you." With this assurance, spoken directly from God, I was able to get to a place where I could declare forgiveness toward my father. That day, God's healing love met me in the midst of a very painful memory.

I have never forgotten this significant moment in my journey of healing and I often reflect on it. God gave me the opposite of what I had received from my earthly father. Instead of anger and rejection, God offered me a deep sense of care—a sense that I was front-and-centre in His eyes, that I was significant to Him, and that I mattered. I knew He would never do anything to hurt me. I heard His heart say, "You can trust Me. You will always be safe with Me."

One Night in Scotland

Shortly after retiring from full-time pastoral ministry a few years ago, I had yet another profound encounter with my Heavenly Father.

Audrey and I had the opportunity to be part of a healing prayer retreat in Scotland where we met with a loving and wise ministry couple who prayed for us to a degree and depth we had never before experienced.

Through this couple's ministry, the Holy Spirit took our lives and years of ministry apart piece by piece, cleaned us up, and put us back together again. No area of our lives were left untouched by the Lord during that time.

The process was sometimes painful, and oftentimes joyful, but totally life-changing. We cried many tears, forgave many people, and found freedom from so many memories and wounds that had accumulated in our lives. I found myself letting go of an identity rooted in my role as a pastor. I moved from being "Pastor Bob" to simply being "beloved son, Bob."

During the retreat, the older gentleman who was ministering to us asked to meet with me. The Lord had told him to impart a father's blessing upon me. He held me in his arms for a long time and spoke words that I had never heard from an older man: "Bob, I'm proud of you. I love you so much. I'm so thankful for who you are, and what you've become, and all you've done." I knew that the words he spoke came directly from the Father's heart and I wept as the healing love of the Father poured into my life.

Later that week, near the end of the retreat, the Lord met me again with an outpouring of His presence. Around midnight, I was in bed listening to praise and worship music when God's presence began to pour over me in what I can only describe as waves of love. Like an incoming tide rolling against a beach, the Father told me how much He loved me, and I told Him how much I loved Him in return.

As this continued into the wee hours of the morning, the sense of His love for me filled my heart to overflowing—so full that I thought I couldn't contain it anymore and my heart would burst. This is among the most powerful encounters of God's love I have ever experienced. Here is an excerpt from my journal, written the next morning:

> Overwhelming sense of God's love for me. My heart bursting with love for Him. Wanting more and more of Him. Wanting to offer my whole self to Him as a complete sacrifice. Caught up into heaven.

What Was Your Father Like?

What was your father like? Was he demanding, distant, angry, abusive, or absent emotionally or physically? Was he withdrawn and reserved, unable to express affection and emotions? Did he ever say "I love you"?

Or was he present and available to you both physically and emotionally? Did he encourage you, support you, and spend time with you? Was he a good example of a godly man, someone you admired and wanted to emulate?

I suspect some of you reading this book grew up in a Christian home and had a good, churchgoing father who lived a respectable life but had little emotional closeness with you.

My wife Audrey grew up with such a father. Like most men of his generation, he never learned how to be affectionate. His love was expressed by working hard and providing for his family. He had two jobs, which meant he was away from home a great deal.

Many men at that time didn't express their emotions openly and freely. Audrey never heard her dad say "I love you" to her. He was active in church life but never engaged emotionally at home. Audrey says the effect of this is that she has had difficulty connecting emotionally to the Heavenly Father's love.

Whether you've grown up with no father, a difficult father, a great father, or anything in

> NO EARTHLY FATHER CAN FULLY MEET OUR DEEPEST LONGING FOR LOVE.

between, we all need to know the love of our Heavenly Father. No earthly father can fully meet our deepest longing for love. No father on earth can do this, nor is one meant to.

A friend of mine calls this the-gap-in-the-program theory, meaning that God intentionally leaves a gap in a child's life that no parent can fill because that gap is meant to be filled with God the Father's love.

While God intends for our earthly fathers to love us well and point us to our Heavenly Father's love, sadly this is not how things often turn out. Most earthly fathers cause some degree of hurt and pain in their children's lives. Sometimes they project their own wounds upon their children, or they are too busy in their own lives to enter the world of their children. Other times, they don't make the effort to listen and understand. Still other times, there is a wall in communication, and the words children need to hear are left unsaid.

However it plays out, all earthly fathers are flawed, broken, and sinful. This is the reason we need an encounter with the love of God, our perfect

Father. As we experience more and more of His love for us and He fills the gap, we will find the deep needs of our heart being met and experience the deepest healing of our hurts.

Dear reader, God wants to stir up this longing within you—a longing for His love and a sense of faith to believe that He is willing and able to meet that longing. In writing my experiences of the Father's love in this chapter, I pray that He will also touch your heart with a desire and hope to encounter His love for you.

Father, thank You for what You have done, and are doing, in my life. Thank You for wanting me to experience a life-changing out-pouring of Your love. I ask You to impart Your love to me in a powerful way—in the way You want for me. Father, may I come to know, by this encounter, that You love me with a love that is wider and longer, and higher and deeper, than I ever thought possible (Ephesians 3:18–19).

In the name of Your Son, Jesus Christ, amen.

Questions for Reflection

1. Describe the family in which you were raised. What was your father like? Your mother? Describe your relationship with your parents, as well as your siblings.
2. What strengths and struggles has your upbringing developed in you?
3. How strong is your longing to feel the Father's love for you and to have a genuine encounter with His love?

The Doorway to the Father

K nowing God is the greatest privilege offered to humanity. How stagger-ing it is to think that God, who is Lord over everything, has made it possible for people to know Him personally!

God, who formed the stars, spoke the universe into being, and now sus-tains all things according to the working of His mighty power, desires a close, personal relationship with each of us. He is the One who sovereignly oversees all of human history with a heart of mercy and commitment to justice. He invites each person to be in a personal relationship with Him as He takes an active interest in our thoughts, circumstances, and feelings. God, who is wor-thy of our utmost adoration and worship, wants to share in our day-to-day, moment-by-moment experiences of life.

What a grand mystery! What a great gift!

I am constantly amazed that God chose to love and rescue me from my own destruction and accept me as one of His beloved children. There really is nothing greater in life than the privilege of intimately knowing God in this way, and this is only possible through the redeeming work of His Son, Jesus Christ.

How could such an intimate relationship be possible unless God made Himself known to us by taking human form? Listen to Jesus's own words:

> *All things have been committed to me by my Father. No one knows who the Son is except the Father, and no one knows who the Father is except the Son and those to whom the Son chooses to reveal him.*
>
> —Luke 10:22

Jesus makes it clear that He is the doorway through which an intimate, restored relationship with the Heavenly Father is possible. He says, *"I am the way and the truth and the life. No one comes to the Father except through me"* (John 14:6).

But to whom does the Son choose to reveal the Father? Is this an exclusive invitation, reserved only for the best behaved, most popular, and most deserving? No, this could not be further from the truth. Jesus's statement of access to the Father is, in fact, an open invitation to all, regardless of any factors they think may disqualify them.

In reading the gospels, we observe Jesus interacting with many people who were rejected or seen as disqualified, either by themselves or by their culture. Jesus paid a great deal of attention to the broken, poor, sinful, cast-aside, and misfit. He went to great lengths to reveal the love of the Father to people—and continues to do so today.

To know Jesus is to know the Father. This is where it all begins. One of Jesus's own disciples, the apostle John wrote, *"We know also that the Son of God [Jesus] has come and has given us understanding, so that we may know him [the Father] who is true"* (1 John 5:20). This reflects a promise made hundreds of years earlier, when Jeremiah prophesied, *"I will give them a heart to know me, that I am the Lord. They will be my people, and I will be their God, for they will return to me with all their heart"* (Jeremiah 24:7).

Observe the language of intimacy used here. *A heart to know me. My people. I will be theirs, they will be mine. Return with all their heart.* This is not the language that many people associate with God, an understanding that is often built around a concept of God as a distant, dominating, or disinterested ruler. This is, rather, the language of the heart-connection that God the Father invites us to enter. God wants us to become fluent in the language of intimacy and to hear His words of love to us.

> GOD WANTS US TO BECOME FLUENT IN THE LANGUAGE OF INTIMACY AND TO HEAR HIS WORDS OF LOVE TO US.

Knowing Christ: Religion vs. Intimacy

A life built upon a religious approach to God is a life with no need for such intimacy. A devoted, religious life characterized by rule-following, role-playing façades, and an emphasis on compliance motivated by a fear of punishment does not require the language of love. Rather, this kind of devotion demands strictness and control through slavish obedience and adherence to impossible standards.

If anyone in biblical history had reason to trust in their religious pedigree, it was Saul, who later became the apostle Paul. Before encountering Christ, Saul was a rigorously trained and devoted Jewish religious leader. Read Paul's self-description in his letter to the Philippians:

> *If someone else thinks they have reasons to put confidence in the flesh, I have more: circumcised on the eighth day, of the people of Israel, of the tribe of Benjamin, a Hebrew of Hebrews; in regard to the law, a Pharisee; as for zeal, persecuting the church; as for righteousness based on the law, faultless.*
>
> —Philippians 3:4–6

People naturally feel good about their religious life when they keep the rules most of the time and consider themselves decent and righteous. A false sense of religious confidence can develop when they perform well in a religious role and compare themselves to other "less devout" people.

In the end, however, as spiritual as this kind of pursuit may seem, Paul makes it clear that these efforts don't produce true righteousness. It only amounts to *"confidence in the flesh"* and endless striving.

Before his conversion, Saul's entire life had been built upon this kind of religious foundation. But everything changed when he had a dramatic encounter with Christ on the road to Damascus (Acts 9). He was blinded by a bright light and heard the thunderous voice of the resurrected Christ.

Saul then came to realize the dead-end road of his religious devotion. Jesus turned Saul's life around and invited him to know God the Father personally. The same God Saul had been seeking to serve and obey through religious rule-keeping was revealed to him as One who intimately loved him and welcomed him into a relationship through Jesus. Saul was offered a new kind of righteousness based on faith in Christ rather than religious performance.

Read the words that immediately follow Paul's self-description in Philippians 3:

But whatever were gains to me I now consider loss for the sake of Christ. What is more, I consider everything a loss because of the surpassing worth of knowing Christ Jesus my Lord, for whose sake I have lost all things. I consider them garbage, that I may gain Christ and be found in him, not having a righteousness of my own that comes from the law, but that which is through faith in Christ—the righteousness that comes from God on the basis of faith.

—Philippians 3:7–9

The Surpassing Worth of Knowing Christ Jesus

I have undergone a similar transformation. As a pastor, I found it easy to adopt a professional orientation in my relationship with God, offering my devotion in return for ministry success. I hoped that the time I spent with God in the scriptures and prayer would result in a good sermon idea, insight into a difficult church problem, or clarity in planning for the future. Blinded by the demands of my work, I was using God to accomplish what I wanted. I was self-serving rather than God-honouring, pursuing a righteousness that centred around me and the fulfillment of my needs in order to validate my performance.

Yet, in an expression of His kindness and love, similar to what He showed to Saul, I encountered Christ in a way that changed the course of my life. The Holy Spirit made me aware of my selfish, sinful motivations and called me to confess these sins and repent. Rather than utilizing guilt and shame, Christ, by His Spirit, told me how much the Father longed to be with me, like a father with a son he loves. The Heavenly Father longed for me to spend time with Him, not for the sake of performance or to seek acceptance, but to simply be with Him, love Him, and connect my heart with His.

Consequently, I experienced a radical change in the way I relate to God. Now my regular practice is to simply *be* with the Lord, primarily but not exclusively through taking time early every morning in prayer and reading the scriptures. In doing these things, I foster a relationship of love with my Heavenly Father—not for what I can get from Him, but because I love and enjoy Him.

Like the apostle Paul, I can say now that knowing Jesus is of far greater worth than any of my religious accomplishments.

My heart goes out to the many church leaders and dedicated volunteers who, like me, have gotten caught in the exhausting treadmill of religious self-effort. My prayer is that God would meet you in the same way He met me and lead you to surrender your need to produce results by your own effort. Allow God to define you first and foremost as His child instead of His worker. Be willing to prioritize spending time with Jesus and pursuing a heart connection. As you do this, you'll find He will bless you and your work will produce the results He wants.

Returning to Where We Belong

Consider God's original design in the Garden of Eden. Adam and Eve literally walked with God and were able to know Him personally and intimately, sharing life together in an unobstructed relationship.

This beautiful relationship broke down when Adam and Eve sinned, resulting in a separation from God that could only be restored through a sacrificial death, which ultimately was the death of Jesus Christ on the cross. That's why Christ died—to bring us back to the Father. God the Father longs for us to reconcile with Him and has made this possible by the work of His Son. He desires to restore our relationship with Him so we can again share life together.

God longs to change lives through a fresh encounter of His love. He desires to meet a core need many people don't even recognize they have. We often want God to simply deal with our problems, for pain to be taken away quickly. We want a quick fix from God rather than allow Him to do a deep work within us.

Instead God wants to draw us into a relational journey with Him of healing and growth, beginning with a revelation of His heart of love for us. He reaches out to us, even in our brokenness and fragmentation, to be our lifelong Friend, not just our Fixer.

My wife and I have listened to hundreds of people's stories, hearing their joys and sorrows as they pour out their hurt and pain. We have observed that while people's problems are often complex and defy simplistic solutions, significant healing is released when they encounter the Father and experience His love for them. We have been privileged to pray with many people and witness the Father's love and healing power flow into them as they choose to become open and willing to receive His love. We have seen some amazing transformations in people as they encounter the Father and sense how much they are loved by Him.

A few years ago, while part of a ministry trip to Belfast, God led me to an older man waiting for prayer ministry. The Holy Spirit whispered to my spirit that this man suffered from a deep father wound in his childhood. I approached him and asked if this was the case. He tearfully poured out his story of hurt and rejection at the hands of his father—of never hearing the words "I love you." He shared how this negatively affected his relationship with his own daughter. He didn't want to repeat the cycle he had experienced with his father.

As we prayed together, God poured His love into this man's heart in such a powerful way that he wept for several minutes. Afterward he told me he had experienced what felt like electric shocks in his body, like a current of love. He could hardly wait to go home and talk to his daughter about the newfound joy, freedom, and deep gratitude he had received during this healing prayer. He was excited to tell his daughter that he loved her and wanted to begin new patterns of relating to her, no longer based on his wounds but on his newfound encounter of the Heavenly Father's love.

Dear reader, God invites you to come close to Him through the doorway of His Son, Jesus Christ. Please join me in this prayer:

Father, I long for You—just for You—because You are all I need. I want to know You more personally and intimately. I want to feel closer and closer to You. Thank You that You long to be close to me. Thank You for making it possible for a way to be opened that connects me with Your heart through Your Son, Jesus.

I love You, Father. When I look back at the end of my life, I want to see that knowing You was the greatest thing—my greatest treasure, joy, and fulfillment. Thank You for creating me to know and love You, not only in this life but more so in the life eternal yet to come.

In Jesus's name, amen.

Questions for Reflection

1. Describe your current relationship with God. Are you more head or heart-oriented? Religious or intimate?

2. How certain are you that you are a genuine child of God who belongs to Him forever? If you're uncertain, what needs to change in order for you to have that certainty?

3. What would you like to change about your relationship with God?

GETTING TO KNOW THE FATHER
Chapter Three

Every morning after getting out of bed, the father would take his cup of tea and go out to the front porch. There he would sit and pray, aching with longing for his youngest son. He would strain his eyes, looking as far down the road as possible, hoping that maybe today he would see his son returning home.

The father began noticing that his vision wasn't what it used to be. Things were getting blurry. The tears didn't help. Some days he thought he saw his son in the distance, but sadly it turned out to be someone else passing by.

Often the father reflected on the recent past. The father knew that life at home was routine, boring, and hard at times, but he had expected both his sons to do their duty while living under his roof. He'd sensed a growing restlessness in his younger son. The young man had seemed to be searching for something new, something better, something exciting. More and more frequently, his son had left for a night or two, sometimes longer.

The father's oldest son certainly knew what was expected of him. He was the model of a hard-working, devoted firstborn—responsible, dependable, living by the rules. The father didn't feel especially close to his oldest son, but he was a faithful and consistent worker. He had what most fathers typically had with their sons, a good working relationship, but not a close, emotional one.

The father still didn't know exactly why he gave in to his younger son's request to receive his full inheritance. It had come as a shock, seemingly out of left field. Already? This soon? What was he planning? The father had thought and prayed about it for a long time and in the end agreed to give him his share of the estate—a significant amount of money, to say the least.

The father remembered the day he announced his decision. "Most sons have to wait for an inheritance, you know. It feels like you're wanting me dead and gone, but I am willing to give it to you. Just remember, this is it. There won't be anything more coming. Use it wisely. I wish you would just stay home and keep working with me and your brother, but I see that your mind is made up and you're determined to leave. I will really miss you."

On the day of his son's departure, the father had stood on this very same porch and watched him leave. His eyes had followed his son as the energetic young man rushed away, not even looking back and waving. The father's heart had been filled with excruciating pain.

Months had passed. Life went on. Work continued.

The other son now seemed to be growing distant and unhappy. Although they never talked about it, the father could tell that his oldest son disagreed with the decision he had made. He sensed the bitterness his older son felt toward both him and his younger brother. Day in and day out, the father and oldest son worked in silence.

Then one morning much like all the rest, as the father watched from his place on the porch, he saw a familiar-looking form far off in the distance. His heart pounded in his chest. He knew that gait, recognized that way of walking.

Yet he couldn't be sure. The man's head was stooped low, his shoulders slumped, the steps tentative. The traveller would sporadically stop as he approached, even sitting down for a while at a certain point, and he seemed confused, unsure. Perhaps he was lost.

For a moment, the father resisted the possibility that this might be his son. He didn't want to be disappointed again if it turned out be another passerby.

But as the figure drew nearer, he clearly saw that his hopes and longings were coming true. It was his beloved son coming home! Had he lost weight? Why did he look so despondent? His clothes looked dirty and his robe was torn. Where were his shoes? Why was his hair so dishevelled?

The father had rehearsed this scene in his mind many times—what he would say to his son. There were several ways this could play out. One was a stern and boisterous rebuke for leaving home, making his son feel the guilt and shame he ought to bear for deserting his father and brother. Another was a cool, distant reception. He would wait and see if his son was appropriately sorry for what he had done. Yet another was a warm welcome to a son who had returned home with a profound and repentant understanding of the error of his ways.

But what happened next surprised even the father.

As the father fully recognized his son, a flood of love and compassion welled up from somewhere deep within his heart. He did something he had never planned. He gathered up the hem of his robe and ran down the road to meet the son he thought he'd lost!

He hadn't run this fast in years. Love fuelled his every step. Nothing else mattered in this moment except the overwhelming need to reach his son and hold him. All the rehearsed speeches and imagined scenes forgotten, the father reached his boy and simply held him, kissed him, and wept.

Initially the younger son resisted his father's embrace. He mumbled something about sinning against God and his father, not deserving to be called a son and some other things. But his speech was cut off by the father, who called for the servants to bring a clean set of clothes and begin preparations for a big feast.

In the embrace of the father, the younger son could only exhale in his weakened state and allow himself to be held.

"This son of mine was dead and gone, but he is alive and home," the father kept saying. "He was lost, but now he is found. He's back. And we're going to celebrate. The only thing we can do is be glad and have a party."

Who the Father Says He Is

The father of the prodigal son presents a clear picture of our Heavenly Father. Let's get to know the Father better as He is revealed in the Bible.

Many people operate out of a faulty understanding of God the Father, an understanding formed from their own experience of pain and lies rather than the clear teaching of scripture and revealing work of the Holy Spirit. These two go hand-in-hand.

> MANY PEOPLE OPERATE OUT OF A FAULTY UNDERSTANDING OF GOD THE FATHER

While an exhaustive scriptural study of the Father is beyond the scope of this book, I want to share some highlights that describe the God of the Bible. Slowly read the following scriptures, pausing to meditate on each statement and what it says about the Heavenly Father. As you do, allow the Holy Spirit to open your heart and mind to more clearly reveal the Father.

Take note of the descriptions of God the Father that resonate with you. Highlight them in this book or make notes in a journal. This is a great starting place in discerning the Holy Spirit's revealing work. Look for words that stir confirmation in your heart ("Yes, I've experienced that!"), a description that evokes a sense of mystery ("Could this really be true?"), or anything that triggers a sense of longing ("Oh, how I long to know a God like this!").

When you're done, take a moment to thank and praise the Father for who He is, what He's like, and what He means to you. As the apostle Paul prayed, *"I keep asking that the God of our Lord Jesus Christ, the glorious Father, may give you the Spirit of wisdom and revelation, so that you may know him better"* (Ephesians 1:17). This is a good prayer for you to pray before engaging in this exercise.

The Father says...

- *"[I am] the Lord, the compassionate and gracious God, slow to anger, abounding in love and faithfulness..."* (Exodus 34:6).
- *"I have loved you with an everlasting love; I have drawn you with unfailing kindness"* (Jeremiah 31:3).
- *"I am the Lord, your Holy One, Israel's Creator, your King"* (Isaiah 43:15).
- *"...I am the Lord, who exercises kindness, justice and righteousness on earth, for in these I delight..."* (Jeremiah 9:24).
- *"[I] forgive all your sins and heal all your diseases... [I redeem] your life from the pit and [crown] you with love and compassion... [I satisfy] your desires with good things so that your youth is renewed like the eagle's"* (Psalm 103:3–5).
- I do not treat you as your *"sins deserve or repay [you] according to [your] iniquities. For as high as the heavens are above the earth, so great is [My] love for those who fear [Me]; as far as the east is from the west, so far [have I] removed [your] transgressions from [you]"* (Psalm 103:10–12).
- I am a merciful Father (Luke 6:36).
- I long *"to be gracious to you... [and will] rise up to show you compassion"* (Isaiah 30:18).

- I am *"a father to the fatherless, and a defender of widows..."* (Psalm 68:5).
- *"As a mother comforts her child, so will I comfort you..."* (Isiah 66:13).
- *"I will lead the blind by ways they have not known, along unfamiliar paths I will guide them; I will turn the darkness into light before them and make the rough places smooth. These are the things I will do; I will not forsake them"* (Isaiah 42:16).
- I reveal *"deep and hidden things... [I know] what lies in darkness, and light dwells with [Me]"* (Daniel 2:22).
- I provide for all your needs (Matthew 6:31–33).
- I am patient and long-suffering (2 Peter 3:9).
- I cause My *"sun to rise on the evil and the good, and [send] rain on the righteous and the unrighteous"* (Matthew 5:45).
- Like a good father, I discipline My children. But My discipline is purely motivated by love and a desire to develop holiness in you (Hebrews 12:5–11).
- My kindness leads you to repentance (Romans 2:4).
- I am unchanging and always consistent (1 Samuel 15:29).
- I am perfect (Matthew 5:48).
- I am beyond understanding (Job 36:26).
- I am *"close to the brokenhearted and... those who are crushed in spirit"* (Psalm 34:18).
- I am a generous Father, a giver of only good gifts (Luke 11:11–12).
- I will give you whatever you ask in the name of My Son, Jesus Christ (John 15:16).
- If you delight in Me, I will *"give you the desires of your heart"* (Psalm 37:4).
- I am the sovereign Lord who *"comes with power, and... rules with a mighty arm"* (Isaiah 40:10).
- I am trustworthy, a promise-keeper, and faithful in all I do (Psalm 145:13).
- I never weary, tire, slumber, or sleep (Psalm 121:4).
- I am always at work (John 5:17).
- I reward *"those who earnestly seek [Me]"* (Hebrews 11:6).

- I lavish My love on you so I can call you My children (1 John 3:1).
- I long for you to *"call me 'Father' and not turn away from following me"* (Jeremiah 3:19).
- *"[I] devise ways so that a banished person does not remain banished from [Me]"* (2 Samuel 14:14).
- *"Even to your old age and grey hairs, I am he. . . who will sustain you. I have made you and I will carry you"* (Isaiah 46:4).
- I am for you and not against you. Nothing can separate you from My love (Romans 8:31, 35).
- I accomplish My purposes. My plans *"stand firm forever, the purposes of [My] heart through all generations"* (Psalm 33:11).
- I poured out all My wrath against sin on Jesus as He hung on the cross (2 Corinthians 5:21).
- I punished Jesus for all your sin (Isaiah 53:4–5).
- I've revealed Myself through My Son, Jesus. You can get to know Me better by looking at His life. Anyone who has seen Jesus has seen Me (John 14:9).

What a great God and Father! Who wouldn't want to know and love a God like this? He has made knowing Him possible through Christ, so that all we need to do now is draw near to Him and spend time with Him. He asks, *"for who is he who will devote himself to be close to me?"* (Jeremiah 30:21).

Let's pray as we close this chapter:

Father, I want to be a person who devotes myself to be close to You. I want to get to know You better. I want to understand and experience Your love. I thank You that You have made it possible through Jesus for me to know You.

Jesus, show me the Father and that will be enough. Reveal to me more of Yourself so I can know and love You in greater ways in the years to come. In Jesus's name, amen.

Questions for Reflection

1. What part of the prodigal son story stood out to you and why?
2. Which descriptions of God the Father caught your attention? Why?
3. Take some time to thank and praise the Father for who He is, what He's like, and what He means to you. Ask Him to meet you in your heart, not just in your mind.

THE FATHER'S *HESED* HEART

Chapter Four

In the process of writing this book, I encountered the Hebrew word *hesed*, as described in a book by Michael Card.[1] The book suggests that this word, simple as it may seem, encapsulates the vast core of God's heart. Becoming familiar with the concept of *hesed* will offer a more vivid understanding of our Heavenly Father and His love for us.

In other words, to understand *hesed* is to begin to understand the Father heart of God.

The Hebrew word *hesed* is used approximately two hundred fifty times throughout the original texts of the Old Testament. This word is so rich with meaning and significance that English translators have grappled with how to appropriately convey the concept. English words fail to properly capture its essence, since there is no direct parallel. Translations of the Bible often attempt to translate *hesed* as love, loyalty, or kindness. But as Michael Card points out,

> One of the fascinating features of *hesed* is its tendency to draw other words to itself by means of its "linguistic gravity." It's as if in struggling to express the inexpressible, the writer [translator] was forced to enlist other words beside *hesed* to help convey its meaning.[2]

As a result, adjectives are often added to establish a stronger understanding, pairings such as: "enduring love," "faithful love," "covenant loyalty," "unswerving loyalty," "merciful love," and "unfailing love." Recent translations of the Bible have frequently landed on the term lovingkindness.

---

1   Michael Card, *Inexpressible: Hesed and the Mystery of God's Loving Kindness* (Downers Grove, IL: InterVarsity Press, 2018).
2   Ibid, 11.

While it's hard to adequately define this ancient word, I have adapted Michael Card's definition to help us in our exploration of the Father heart of God: "*Hesed* is when God, from whom I deserve nothing, gives me everything."[3]

Think about it. What do we deserve from God? Because of our sin, we deserve nothing good, only wrath, condemnation, and eternal separation from Him. But what does God give us instead? Mercy, forgiveness, love, and eternal life.

In a significant Self-revelation on Mount Sinai, God tells Moses that *hesed* is one of His major defining qualities. After God placed Moses in a cleft of the rock and covered him with His hand, He passed by in all His glory and proclaimed His name: *"The Lord, the Lord, the compassionate and gracious God, slow to anger, abounding in love [hesed] and faithfulness..."* (Exodus 34:6) These words help define God's *hesed* heart.

Card provides a Father heart insight when he points out that in Exodus 34:6, the first word God uses to define Himself is *compassionate*:

> ...the Hebrew word for *compassion* in this verse is similar to the word used for *womb* and implies the love elicited to a helpless baby from a mother or father. Though He has yet to reveal Himself as Father, the first word used by God to describe His character is a parental word.[4]

This is an early foreshadowing of the Father-heart of God, which only grows stronger throughout the scriptures.

Hesed in the Old Testament

Consider the story of Adam and Eve as an example of God's *hesed*. They chose to disobey God in the Garden of Eden by eating from the tree of the knowledge of good and evil, an expressly prohibited action. Even though they suffered the consequences of their disobedience, God, in His *hesed*, provided for their needs and ultimately made a covenant of unfailing mercy and faithfulness to future generations.

---

3   Ibid, 5.
4   Ibid, 23.

Jonah, the prophet who fled in the opposite direction from God's call, became a fugitive, taking passage on a ship to a faraway destination. He ended up being thrown into the stormy sea, given up for dead. But because of *hesed*, God arranged for a large fish to swallow him and return him to dry land, giving Jonah a second chance at obedience.

By God's choice and anointing, David became a mighty warrior and great king. Yet with all his privilege, David committed the grievous sin of adultery and murder, resulting in the death of the child he had conceived with Bathsheba. David then humbly and sincerely confessed his sin and repented before the Lord. Despite suffering harsh consequences, God, in His *hesed*, forgave David and continued to bless and work through him, his descendants, and all who would choose to take the same humble-hearted posture.

Consider Ruth, a foreigner from Moab and young widow who, having lost her husband and the rights that came with that, chose to care for her widowed mother-in-law Naomi. Together, these two refugees travelled back to Naomi's homeland in Judah and attempted to start over, despite the prejudices held by the local Israelites towards people from Moab. In this new environment, Ruth experienced God's *hesed* through an act of mercy by a "kinsman redeemer" named Boaz. He chose to marry Ruth in order to start a new family with her, establishing a place of security and belonging for both Ruth and her mother-in-law.

Hesed is not only learned through stories in the Old Testament; it is also meant to evoke an emotional response in us, to incite grateful worship.

Interestingly, among all the books in the Old Testament, the one that uses the word *hesed* most is the book of Psalms. This worship and prayerbook invites us not only to be observers of *hesed*, but also to respond and participate in the very nature of God Himself. Here are two examples:

> . . .*for I have always been mindful of your unfailing love and have lived in reliance on your faithfulness.*
>
> —Psalm 26:3

> *Because your love is better than life, my lips will glorify you.*
>
> —Psalm 63:3

The Old Testament paints a picture of a God who is gracious and compassionate, slow to anger, and abounding in love (Psalm 86:15). A God who goes to great lengths to usher His people into the experience of life He has always intended for them. A God whose focus on the heart always supersedes His focus on external action, sinful or religious.

Even in God's harshness and anger, His *hesed* can be found. The psalmist says, *"For His anger lasts only a moment, but his favour* [hesed] *lasts a lifetime"* (Psalm 30:5).

Hesed in the New Testament

The concept and language of *hesed* isn't limited to the Old Testament. In the New Testament, the term is brought into a new and sharpened focus. Here, *hesed* is shown through the Person and teachings of Jesus Christ. The original texts of the New Testament convey the concept of *hesed* with the Greek word *eleos*, meaning "mercy."

Jesus's story of the prodigal son, as retold in the previous chapter, is a beautiful example of this sharpened understanding. The younger son in the story deserved nothing from his father. He didn't deserve to be welcomed home with open arms after squandering his share of the inheritance. He didn't deserve to be restored as a privileged son after such willful disobedience. He didn't deserve to be celebrated with such joy after causing so much grief. Yet, in deserving nothing, he received everything—kindness instead of anger, mercy instead of judgment, forgiveness instead of condemnation, and restoration instead of rejection.

This story would have been quite an insult to Jesus's Jewish listeners, who had been conditioned to build their lives on unrelenting religious demands and a concept of a God who could only be pleased with perfect obedience. In the minds of Jesus's first listeners, the younger son should have been written off by the father and certainly not welcomed back. "Get out! You've made your choice. Now live with the consequences. You aren't worthy to be called my son anymore!"

Instead, Jesus's story paints a powerful picture of the true *hesed* heart of God the Father, who gives undeserving mercy (*eleos*) to all who come to Him in a posture of humble repentance. They receive God's undeserved gift of love, welcome, and acceptance.

Jesus presents a true and accurate picture of God in this story. Jesus, who was in His very nature God, sought to reorient His lost, religious culture to the truth of who God is. Instead of being the overbearing taskmaster, God was shown to be the merciful and loving Father, the same Father to whom Jesus instructed His disciples to pray, the same Father to whom He called out with His last breath on the cross.

This sharpened understanding of *hesed* became the central picture of God to shape the early Christian church. In writing to a fledgeling community of Christ-followers in Rome, Paul used striking language that harkened back to Jesus's own depiction of God:

> So you have not received a spirit that makes you fearful slaves. Instead, you received God's Spirit when he adopted you as his own children. Now we call him, "Abba, Father." For his Spirit joins with our spirit to affirm that we are God's children.
> —Romans 8:15–16, NLT

Hesed in Our World Today

We find a *hesed* story in the account of Sharletta Evans from Denver, Colorado. Her three-year-old son Casson was killed by a teenager named Raymond Johnson in a drive-by shooting.

Johnson had grown up in a troubled home and found his way to the streets where gang violence was a way of life. He and a fellow gang member sprayed bullets into a parked car where Casson was sleeping while his mother was picking up another child from a duplex. Johnson, fifteen at the time, was sentenced to life behind bars.

While in prison, Johnson wrote to Sharletta expressing his deep remorse and asking her to reach out to him. After some time and inner struggle, Sharletta agreed to meet with him through a prison program called Restorative Justice.

Their first meeting lasted eight hours. Sharletta described this encounter with Johnson as "everything I had hoped for." That meeting set the stage for many more encounters between the convicted killer and his victim's mother.

As time went on, Sharletta found herself experiencing a growing compassion and forgiveness towards this broken young man. She said, "I can truly say I love the young man and love him enough to take him as a son and care for him."

In December 2021, Johnson was released from prison and planned to start a program focusing on reducing youth violence, a program he dedicated to Casson.[5]

How unlikely and counterintuitive—the grieving parent of a murdered child who became willing not only to forgive the murderer, but also to invite him to become part of her family.

What could possibly determine such an outcome, and why does a story like this stir up such a range of emotions in people's hearts? Because it is an outbreaking of *hesed*, the very nature of God in His mercy and love being put on display against all odds.

A *Hesed* Husband

I will never forget the story of a dear older couple in one of the churches I pastored. He was an academic at the university, and she had been a nurse. Both were highly intelligent and accomplished people.

Sadly, the wife struggled with mental illness. She was full of fear, experienced depression, remained extremely isolated, and had difficulty showing affection. She had suffered a great deal of trauma in her childhood and, despite many attempts at offering help, she was unwilling to open up about it to anyone in order to find healing.

I took many phone calls from the husband, worried sick, telling me that his wife had left home without telling anyone where she was going. On most occasions she'd be gone for a day, sometimes two, but when she came home she wouldn't say where she had been. This behaviour intensified as the years progressed.

---

5 "'We Can Redeem Ourselves': Mother's Loss Transformed as She Forgives Gunman Who Shot, Killed Her Son," *CBS News*. December 21, 2021 (https://www.cbsnews.com/colorado/news/sharletta-evans-raymond-johnson-casson-evans-deadly-shooting).

The one bright spot in this sad situation was her husband's response. Throughout their marriage, which lasted more than fifty years, he treated her with kindness, care, compassion, and forgiveness—a *hesed* type of love.

Even when she came back from one of her mystery trips and wouldn't give him any explanation, he welcomed her home with open arms. His love for her was loyal, faithful, and completely devoted. He sacrificed a great deal in his professional career in order to care for her, but he never resented it. Right to the end of her life, when she was nonverbal and living in a care home with dementia, he visited her every day, showing his love and tenderness to her.

Being a young husband at the time, I observed this godly example and was deeply inspired to model the same in my own marriage—to respond to my family members with abundant kindness and love, even when their behaviour didn't deserve it. This is another picture of God's *hesed* love—when someone from whom I deserve nothing gives me everything.

As we grow in our understanding of *hesed*, we experience a change in the way we relate to our Heavenly Father. When we begin to grasp the incredible depths of

> AS WE GROW IN OUR UNDERSTANDING OF *HESED*, WE EXPERIENCE A CHANGE IN THE WAY WE RELATE TO OUR HEAVENLY FATHER.

His undeserved mercy and the great lengths He goes in order to extend it to those who are undeserving, how can a profound sense of gratitude not rise up from deep within us? How can we resist the opportunity to love, obey, and serve this amazing God who loves us, has forgiven us, and has shown mercy to us when we deserved the exact opposite?

A growing understanding of *hesed* propels us into a greater experience of prayer, inviting us to approach the throne of grace with increased boldness and confidence *"so that we may receive mercy and find grace to help us in our time of need"* (Hebrews 4:16).

As Michael Card writes,

> The person who understands the *hesed* of God is always ready to persistently ask, seek and knock on the door that opens up to a world of promise they have done nothing to deserve. As we come

to understand God's *hesed* we will have a growing confidence that He is delighted to give us His blessings.[6]

Pray now with me, dear reader:

Father, thank You for Your hesed *heart. Thank You for not treating me as my sins deserve, but freely offering me mercy, love, kindness, and forgiveness. Thank You that I can trust Your* hesed *heart and place my life fully in Your care. You are a good Father and I want to get to know and trust You more all the days of my life. In Jesus's name, amen.*

Questions for Reflection

1. Consider the definition of *hesed* given in this chapter. How do you understand this definition? How does the concept of *hesed* impact you?
2. In what ways have you experienced *hesed* love from God and others?
3. What would it look like for you to show *hesed* to someone else?

---

6   Card, *Inexpressible*, 112.

THE WORDS WE LONG TO HEAR

Chapter Five

There is a longing in every person's heart to know that they are loved—that they matter to someone, that they're valued and cherished, that someone considers them important. Everyone wants to hear these things from the significant people in their lives.

This is especially true between a child and their parents. God's design is that a child be nurtured in a caring family where love is communicated in every way possible, through words and actions.

Growing up fatherless, I never heard loving words from a father figure and I've suffered because of this. Thankfully, my mom often told me she loved me.

That is why I determined, when I was a young father, that my children would hear these important words from me often—and not only hear them, but see them demonstrated in my actions.

I have loved being a dad through every stage of my children's lives, from playing with them in their young imaginary worlds to attending their concerts, games, and events, going on spontaneous dates, and just hanging out. I have found great delight in supporting them as they cultivated their gifts, skills, interests, and callings. Despite some hard times, mistakes, and failures on my part, being a dad is one of the greatest joys of my life! And now being a grandfather is the icing on the cake.

I am mentoring a young man who has two young boys. This father is struggling to connect deeply with the love of the Heavenly Father. His story is similar to mine in that he also grew up fatherless and is searching for a faithful father's love.

I asked him to write a letter to his sons, telling them from his heart how much he loves them and what they mean to him. I prayed that as he composed this letter, he would hear his Heavenly Father speak these same words to him. Here's what he wrote:

Dear sons,

It is my greatest joy to be in your presence. It is an honour, privilege, and great pleasure to provide, watch over, and guide you. It is easy to live in the moment with you and be fully present and intentional. I feel like I have risen to my best with you. I adore the sound of your voices and love the touch of your clammy little hands. I love your slobbery kisses and your tight hugs. I love your silly run, your one-sided crawl. I love the sound of your tiny feet thumping around the house.

Always be you. Your big blue eyes and pure smiles wreck me daily. The sound of your laughter is like heavenly music. You are my sunshine. Nothing you do could make me love you less or more. You are mine, my boys, my loves. I am proud of you. You are the most remarkable, splendid, wonderful, and magnificent beings God has ever created. You are my reason for being. My life's work, my ultimate creation.

Love, Dad

Can you imagine what a powerful impact this letter will have on those boys when they are able to read it for themselves?

The Heavenly Father is saying words like these to you and has been since you were born. He fashioned every detail about you in your mother's womb.

For you created my inmost being; you knit me together in my mother's womb. I praise you because I am fearfully and wonderfully made; your works are wonderful, I know that full well. My frame was not hidden from you when I was made in the secret place, when I was woven together in the depths of the earth. Your eyes saw my unformed body; all the days ordained for me were written in your book before one of them came to be. How precious to me are your thoughts, God! How vast is the sum of them!

—Psalm 139:13–17

The Heavenly Father wants His words of love and blessing to meet the deepest longings of your heart. He is no stranger to speaking words of blessing to His children. As a matter of fact, He spoke significant words to His own Son on the occasion of His baptism and the start of His public ministry.

Jesus was baptized in the Jordan River by His cousin, John the Baptist. When He came up out of the water, heaven was opened and He saw the Spirit of God descending like a dove and landing on Him. Then He heard His Father's voice from heaven saying these life-giving words: *"This is my Son, whom I love; with him I am well pleased"* (Matthew 3:17).

In this moment, the Father publicly declared Jesus's identity as His beloved Son. The Heavenly Father put His stamp of approval on Jesus as He began His public ministry, with His Father's help and blessing. The Father audibly spoke His love and affirmation.

Think about it. Before Jesus performed any public miracles, the Father told Him that He was a beloved Son. Period. He had nothing to prove. There was only unconditional love and acceptance. Jesus's standing with the Father wasn't based on His performance, but on His relationship with the Father.

These are the words we all long to hear from the Father. And we can.

Here's the good news: what the Father said to Jesus, He is saying to you. He is saying, "You are My son, My daughter, whom I love; with you I am well pleased." He longs for you to hear these words and really believe them.

Read those words again. Say them out loud. Add your name to them. Make it personal, like it's become to me: "Bobby, you are My beloved son. I love you. I am well pleased with you."

These words, spoken directly from the Father's heart, have the power to shape us into secure, joyful, empowered, deeply loved children of God. But for that to happen, these words have to touch us in the deep places of our heart.

This is where the ministry of the Holy Spirit enters the picture. He will take these words and plant them deeply in our hearts if we ask Him to.

Paul reminds us of the Spirit's work in Romans 8:16: *"The Spirit himself testifies with our spirit that we are God's [beloved, well-pleasing] children"* (Romans 8:16).

These may be the most important words we can ever hear from the Father. Many people are still trying to earn the Father's love and approval by what they do for Him. I know; I'm one of them. Deep in the broken places of our hearts, we still think we have to prove something to Him about who we are and what we can do. We think God will be pleased with us when we serve Him well and displeased when we don't. So much of our service for God is motivated by insecurity, doubt, fear, and the lie that God's love is conditional on how well we perform.

In contrast, before the start of His public ministry, Jesus was given the gift of His Father's absolute love and approval. For the next three years, Jesus was free to serve His Father from a place of belonging, acceptance, and security. He didn't work *for* God's approval, but *from* God's approval. He was never unsure about what His Father thought of Him, or whether He was doing enough, or doing things right. He was absolutely settled in the love of His Father and able to live out of His identity.

You and I need to hear the Father's voice saying the same thing to us—and we need to hear it often. We need to hear it again and again because we tend to drift into doubt and insecurity. It can take time for life-changing truths to seep into our hearts and take a firm hold.

Consider this. The Father doesn't just say He is pleased with us; He says He is well pleased. More than pleased. Beyond pleased. It is wonderful enough to be called pleasing to God, but He says that we are super-pleasing to Him. Astonishing!

While many people accept the "whom I love" part, they have trouble with the "well pleased" part, especially at an emotional level. They have difficulty believing that God would say this about them, knowing all too well the true condition of their lives. They only see their sins, mistakes, rebellion, and brokenness. They are not pleased with themselves. They also remember the hurtful words of displeasure others have spoken to them. They wonder, *How can God be well pleased with someone like me? Certainly Jesus deserved these words, but I sure don't.*

> THE FATHER IS WELL PLEASED WITH JESUS AND THEREFORE IS WELL PLEASED WITH YOU.

The truth of how much we please the Father must be settled biblically before it can be accepted emotionally. That's why some people have trouble believing it. The biblical understanding we need is this: the Father is well pleased with Jesus and therefore is well pleased with you.

God's favour and pleasure with you has nothing to do with who you are or what you have done. It has nothing to do with how good or bad you are. It has everything to do with Jesus, who He is and what He has done.

Because we are in Christ and our life is hidden with Him (Colossians 3:3), what is true of Jesus is also true of us. As Christians, we have been justified by faith in Christ, and our right standing with God depends on Christ's righteousness and not our own. The Father sees each of us through Jesus, who took our punishment for sin and has clothed us in His righteousness. On this biblical basis, then, we can legitimately be declared well pleasing to the Father.

If you're one of those people who find themselves on an endless treadmill of trying harder to do all the right things so God will be pleased with you, I urge you to stop and talk to God about it right now. Ask Him to show you why. Why are you driven to perform? Are you trying to earn something that is already freely available to you in Christ? Are you trying to prove something to yourself, others, or God? For whom are you performing?

As God reveals any sinful core motivations, it will be necessary to repent, turn away from them, and embrace the truth of your status as God's beloved, well pleasing child. What a joy to live with nothing to prove to yourself, God, or anyone else! Let the Father know that you desire a settled experience of His love in the same way Jesus did, and that you long to hear His voice saying that you are His beloved child with whom He is well pleased.

Then wait quietly in His presence and listen to what He will say to you. Don't give up if you don't hear anything from God right away. We can't force the Father to speak whenever we want. He is sovereign, good, and kind and knows what we need. But more importantly, He knows when we need it. God knows the right time and best way for us to receive a revelation of His love that will meet our deepest need. We must learn to be still before Him (Psalm 46:10) and present ourselves to Him with longing and expectation, trusting Him to pour out His words of affirmation upon us at just the right time.

The Father Who Sings Over Us

Many parents have memories of singing to their small children while holding them in their arms. These are tender moments of love, strengthening the parent/child bond.

Did you know that your Heavenly Father sings over you? He loves to sing songs over you. Listen to what the Old Testament prophet Zephaniah says:

The Lord your God is with you, the Mighty Warrior who saves. He will take great delight in you; in his love he will no longer rebuke you, but will rejoice over you with singing.

—Zephaniah 3:17

Take a moment to imagine this lovely scene. Let yourself feel His strong arms cradling you close to His heart. Feel His embrace. See Him looking into your face and smiling. Look into His eyes and see the adoring love they display. Picture Him singing a tender song over you. Perhaps the lyrics are the very words we long to hear about being His beloved child whom He loves, with whom He is well pleased. Feel the love radiating from His heart.

What are you feeling? Can you feel the peace, safety, warmth, complete rest, the freedom from every care? What other feelings do you have?

The Father wants us to see Him with the eyes of our heart. When we do, it becomes easier to hear those words: "You are My son, My daughter, whom I love. With you I am well pleased."

Dear reader, may you hear these words from the Father's heart spoken to you many, many times. Here's a prayer for you:

Father, thank You that I am Your beloved child, whom You love, with whom You are well pleased. I want to hear it, believe it, and receive it. May your Holy Spirit open the eyes and ears of my heart so these words will take root and form me into a flourishing child of Yours.

I long for that quiet place of settled love where I can rest and wait to hear Your voice. I know that place is found in You. Help me grow and flourish as Your deeply loved child. Thanks for being my Father, whom I love.

In Jesus's name, amen.

Questions for Reflection

1. "You are My Son, My daughter, whom I love; with you I am well pleased." How do these words from the Father impact you? How would your life be different if these words took firm hold in your heart and mind? Tell the Father how much you long to hear these words directly from Him.

2. Do you believe that the Father is well pleased with you? Why or why not?

3. How often do you find yourself on the performance treadmill, trying to please God by working hard for Him? Ask God to show you why you're driven to perform for God's approval.

4. What steps do you need to take to get off the performance treadmill?

REAL ARMS
Chapter Six

A few years ago, Audrey and I met with a wonderful Christian couple for prayer at their request. The woman in particular had a sincere longing to experience the Father's love; it was a desperate desire to feel His love in a genuine way.

She was a long-term, devoted follower of Jesus. I had been her pastor for several years and knew how sincere and committed she and her husband were. This woman served faithfully in the church and met with the Lord regularly in her private times in the Word and prayer. She loved the Lord and His people and was a grounded, sensible person.

Like many Christians, she had a foundational knowledge of God's love—it existed in her head—but she rarely, if ever, felt it in her heart. This dear woman was hungry for more. She wanted to experience the Father's love. She wanted to connect with Him at a heart level and feel His deep love for her, not just settle for mere intellectual understanding.

We spent time listening to her story and engaged in prayer ministry for her and her husband, asking God to pour out His love in their hearts.

The following account, written by her and used with her permission, describes what happened later that night when she returned home from our meeting.

I was praying in the living room that night, and I asked the Lord to show me His heart and His love for me. Very soon, I felt that He was standing behind the sofa I was sitting on and leaned down to put His arms around my shoulders in a tender hug. It was so real. It actually felt tangible. Real arms! He stayed there for quite a while and just let me soak in His gentle outpouring of tenderness. I was utterly immersed in His love and felt like a sponge, simply absorbing as much as I possibly could. I still get teary just thinking about it… how merciful of Him to do that!

After some time I crawled into bed, thanking God for meeting me in a way that revealed His love so unmistakably. If I remember correctly, I was praising Him and asking Him to grant me language to praise Him more deeply if and when He chose.

At any rate, I almost immediately received two syllables of a new spiritual language which I tried out, not completely sure I was hearing right. But it seemed appropriate, so I whispered them over and over. The Lord was very present in that moment and I was totally basking in His glory.

Not long thereafter, I received a third syllable. This seemed to clinch something… like completing a sentence. As I murmured my three syllables, it was if He came closer and closer and closer. It's impossible to describe the depth of it, but I was utterly awash with praise, flooded with love. Not one cell of my being was left out…

It's hard to believe but it gets even better!

At some point during this time of praise—I struggle to find the words to describe it—I was invited directly into the heart of God. I don't know how else to say it. It felt like I was inside a cave. One that was just big enough to comfortably curl up in, and surrounded by the softest, plushest material ever. And what filled me was even more precious than what surrounded me!

I was helpless to do anything but praise (and that's all I wanted to do), still repeating my three syllables over and over. Their meaning somehow conveyed the greatest sense of adoration. Never have I felt so clearly connected to my purpose and I wanted to keep going forever. Nothing else mattered. I was drawn in and shown love like I've never known, and I was also reflecting it back as intensely as I could.

I can only imagine that this may have been a taste of what we will experience when we are actually in the presence of Jesus for eternity. I can't wait! This unbelievable experience lasted at least two hours. Eventually I fell asleep praising my King. Unbelievable!

I believe this was one of those experiences that stays with you and shapes you and keeps you afloat for the rest of your time on earth. The God of the universe cradled me in His heart! Whenever I sit and ponder this, I weep. Even now I have tears in my eyes.

Similar to what my friend experienced, I believe God the Father wants to give us all a tangible experience of His love, one that is perfectly designed for our unique personality and emotional makeup. He will give us what we need in a way we can receive it. After all, God is the one who designed us. He knows exactly how to touch us at the deepest level.

How Do People Experience the Father's Love?

During the writing of this book, I became keenly interested in how other people experience God's love and how they describe it. I asked a number of people who I know and trust, and who have a genuine heart-relationship with the Heavenly Father, to tell me about their experiences. Their responses are varied and inspiring.

Below are a number of stories from men and women of different ages, stages, and walks of life. Read about how they describe their experience of what it feels like for them to encounter the Father's love.

I feel the Father's love coursing through me most intimately in those moments when He breaks through to me. In those moments, all I can do is stop what I am doing and hunch over while deep, heaving sobs rack my body and my deepest inner being releases whispers of thanksgiving for His mercy and grace in and through my life.

Caring, gentleness, joy, and encouragement. Snuggled into his lap, His arms enfold me like a loving Father. I feel overwhelmingly loved and protected. He is the provider of all my needs.

To be loved by God is realizing that He is always for me, and is working out His best in every situation. It's living under His smile of pure delight in me, knowing that He is fully present and ready to be whatever I need in every situation.

I feel safe and secure no matter the situation, and I am confident of His loving presence.

It is comforting to know that God is always there for me, accepts me for who I am, and wants to bring me into the best He has for me. I feel His peace and strength.

I feel His presence occasionally as a physical weight. I feel like I'm not alone. I feel a sense of peace and confidence.

For me, the love of God feels like a promise... a very personal, sacred promise of acceptance which can never be revoked or withdrawn. The promise is invitational. It is trustworthy and it is completely relational. As I bask in the promise, I feel remarkably valued and that my life matters.

At a prayer evening, a pastor publicly said he had a word from the Lord for me. He then read Psalm 45:10–11 and prayed over me! I was able to release my burdens for my prodigal son and also my marriage into my Father's care. I could feel the Holy Spirit enveloping me and pouring His love into me. I experienced God's love so intensely that it changed my life!

My emotional experience of the Father's love for me feels like a deep joy and contentment. This typically happens in the simplest moments—observing the intricacy, colour, and fragrance from a flower; receiving a warm, genuine embrace from a loved one; having a mutual guffaw with someone who accepts me fully. If I notice the moment that is reflecting God's love for me, those feelings of joy and contentment run deep and keep me going on this journey.

For me, I can feel God's love burn like a flame inside my chest. It keeps me warm when I'm cold, comforts me when I'm lonely, and guides me when I'm lost. It is a gentle embrace, full of love.

Through God's Word, His people, and His creation, there comes an overwhelming sense of His all-encompassing presence—companionship, strength, comfort, guidance, wisdom, joy, and refreshment. It is at the same time tenderly gentle and powerful, with a knowledge that I am not alone, that He is deeply vested in all things, present in my life.

When I think about being loved, I imagine crawling up into Jesus's lap and feeling His arms holding me tight as I snuggle in for a hug. I can just feel His peace, and His smile, and His joy filling me.

I feel the love of God through the warmth of His embrace when I mess up. I know He loves me always and is not happy I mess up, but He is not critical of me either. He shows me His unconditional love over and over again, and this brings me confidence to call Him "Father."

How would you answer the question of what it feels like to experience the Father's love? What testimony can you give about your experience of His love? I pray that as you continue to read this book, your testimony of the Father's love will grow stronger and become a vital, life-giving inspiration to many.

A Letter from the Father

Several years ago, in the conclusion to a sermon on hearing the Father's voice, I challenged our congregation to take time to listen to what the Father was saying to them and write it down.

A close friend and someone I consider a spiritual son wrote the following in the form of a letter from the Heavenly Father to him:

Dear son,

I just want to affirm to you again today that you are precious to Me. I am proud of the man you have become and your willingness to become a better person. You have loved Me from your younger years and are always a useful instrument in my hands. I made you distinctive among your siblings, exalting you above your peers. I have blessed you with a wife and children for you to continue to show them love and lead them in My way.

Do not be afraid. I will make all provisions available for you to be the godly father I desire you to be and your home will be an example to many. I will instruct you in the way you should go and show you the way everlasting.

You are forever precious to me and I love you with My everlasting love.

Love, your Dad, Almighty God

Experiencing the Father's love is uniquely personal and intimate. Many people long for this reality. God is inviting you to experience His love in ways you have never known before.

Dear reader, take some time now to sit with the Father and ask Him to communicate His heart to you—to impress His immense love upon your heart and mind. Write down what you think He might be saying. This practice is not some form of high-level spirituality but something every child of God is able to experience. It simply requires stillness and faith to believe that the Father wants and is eager to communicate with those He loves. The Father is not stingy, reserving His voice for perfect people or perfect circumstances. He is eager to engage with anyone who is willing to listen with expectation. You can hear His voice!

Pray now with me:

Loving Father, I long to experience Your love in a real and tangible way. I open my heart wide to You. Meet me, touch me, speak to me, and fill me with Your love. Increase my longing for an experience of Your love.

In the words of Psalm 63:1, "You, God, are my God, earnestly I seek you; I thirst for you, my whole being longs for you, in a dry

and parched land where there is no water." *Hold me in Your arms, Your real arms. Gather me in Your arms and carry me close to Your heart. I love You, Father! I really do love You!*
In Jesus's name, amen.

Questions for Reflection

1. What part of the opening story in the chapter stands out to you and why?

2. Write a two or three sentence answer to this question: what does it feel like to be loved by God?

3. Take some time to sit quietly with the Father and ask Him to show you His heart, to pour out His love upon you. Isaiah 40:11 says, *"He tends his flock like a shepherd: he gathers the lambs in his arms and carries them close to his heart; he gently leads those that have young"* (Isaiah 40:11). Don't rush through this time, but linger in His presence. Describe your experience.

THE ABBA FATHER CRY

Chapter Seven

The truth at the heart of this book is that our Heavenly Father greatly desires a tender and personal love relationship with us. He calls us His children and wants us to call Him Abba Father.

The Aramaic word Abba is a child-like, tender term used by children in that culture when addressing their father. Abba is a term of endearment, a desire for personal, intimate connection full of love and a longing for closeness. A close English equivalent would be Dada, Daddy, or Papa. These terms are best imagined in conjunction with arms outstretched—a child wanting to be held. This cry expresses a beautiful dependence on a father's help and care.

The key to understanding and engaging with the Father's love in this way is found in Paul's letter to the Romans. Here is the clearest and most significant passage of scripture having to do with what I refer to as the Abba Father cry:

> *You, however, are not in the realm of the flesh but are in the realm of the Spirit, if indeed the Spirit of God lives in you. And if anyone does not have the Spirit of Christ, they do not belong to Christ. But if Christ is in you, then even though your body is subject to death because of sin, the Spirit gives life because of righteousness. And if the Spirit of him who raised Jesus from the dead is living in you, he who raised Christ from the dead will also give life to your mortal bodies because of his Spirit who lives in you.*
>
> *Therefore, brothers and sisters, we have an obligation—but it is not to the flesh, to live according to it. For if you live according to the flesh, you will die; but if by the Spirit you put to death the misdeeds of the body, you will live.*
>
> *For those who are led by the Spirit of God are the children of God. The Spirit you received does not make you slaves, so that you live in fear again; rather, the Spirit you received brought about your adoption to sonship [daughtership].*

And by him we cry, "Abba, Father." The Spirit himself testifies with our spirit that we are God's children. Now if we are children, then we are heirs—heirs of God and co-heirs with Christ, if indeed we share in his sufferings in order that we may also share in his glory.

—Romans 8:9–17

A Work of the Holy Spirit

The Abba Father cry can best be described as a Spirit-given longing for the loving presence of the Heavenly Father. As we will see, it comes from deep within our hearts and expresses closeness, tenderness, trust, and dependency on our Father. The Holy Spirit moves in each individual heart, knowing how to best teach a person this cry. There is no one way to express the Abba Father cry.

It is important to note in these verses from Romans 8 that the impulse to cry out to God as Abba Father comes from a work of the Holy Spirit. Take note of how greatly the work of the Spirit is highlighted throughout this chapter. The Holy Spirit is the One who enables us to both receive the Father's love and offer our love back to Him. Engaging with the Father's love is not something we can participate in by our own means.

We can't depend on knowledge alone to engage with God's love. Religious practice and adherence to tradition won't get us there. We can't deny ourselves enough, read enough, or pray enough to establish this intimate connection.

What we need is the Holy Spirit to give us a revelation of the Father's love. The Holy Spirit joins our hearts with His and produces this cry deep within us. Knowledge informs, but revelation transforms. Spiritual disciplines prepare us as vessels to receive God's love, but the Holy Spirit pours it into us.

The Development of the Abba Father Cry

Notice how the Romans 8 passage presents the development of the Abba Father cry in a very particular order.

I. Becoming a true child of God. The first and most essential place to begin is to know with certainty that we are genuine sons and daughters of God. This is validated by the presence of the indwelling Holy Spirit.

> *You, however, are not in the realm of the flesh but are in the realm of the Spirit, if indeed the Spirit of God lives in you. And if anyone does not have the Spirit of Christ, they do not belong to Christ.*
>
> —Romans 8:9

As a first step in this journey, the Holy Spirit must reside in us in order for us to fully experience the Father's love and the Abba Father cry.

We must first know with certainty that we are children of God and a part of His family, and that God is our Father and Jesus Christ our Saviour. We must know with certainty that Jesus Christ is the one and only Person who can reconcile our separation from the Heavenly Father, caused by our sin (Romans 3:23).

To enter into this relationship, you need to *"declare with your mouth, 'Jesus is Lord,' and believe in your heart that God raised him from the dead"* (Romans 10:9). You must know that you have been saved by grace through faith in Jesus Christ, and not by depending on your own good works (Ephesians 2:8–9). You must place your faith in Jesus Christ alone for salvation, believing that He is the only way, the truth, and the life, and *"no one comes to the Father except through [Him]"* (John 14:6).

2. Being led by the Holy Spirit. Secondly, we are called to become children of God who are led by the Spirit.

> *Therefore, brothers and sisters, we have an obligation—but it is not to the flesh, to live according to it. For if you live according to the flesh, you will die; but if by the Spirit you put to death the misdeeds of the body, you will live.*
> *For those who are led by the Spirit of God are the children of God.*
>
> —Romans 8:12–14

Instead of being led by our sinful desires and human impulses, we are to be led and controlled by the Spirit of God. As a matter of fact, it is so important for us to live lives controlled by the Spirit of God that Paul establishes this as a defining characteristic of a true child of God.

Being led by the Holy Spirit means we will experience freedom from the control of sin. Paul makes it clear that the Holy Spirit is the one who sets us free from slavery to sin and self. In other words, the Holy Spirit sets us free from slavery to anything—our fears, addictions, false self, or whatever it is that tries to hold us captive.

The leadership of the Holy Spirit also enables us to sustain a journey of walking in God's ways rather than our own ways, which often lead to unnecessary confusion and pain. Paul urges us to *"walk by the Spirit, and you will not gratify the desires of the flesh"* (Galatians 5:16).

Whenever I read the phrase "walk by the Spirit," I picture a deep snowfall and a young child following in her father's footsteps. She hops from one deep footprint to the next, walking where her father walked, enabling her to make her way through the deep snow. We are encouraged by Paul to keep in step with the Spirit in the same way.

3. Adoption. Thirdly, the Spirit transacts our adoption as sons and daughters of God.

> *The Spirit you received does not make you slaves, so that you live in fear again; rather, the Spirit you received brought about your adoption to sonship [daughtership]. . .*
> —Romans 8:15

The word adoption in the New Testament means being placed as an orphaned child into a family.

Paul explains to us that the Holy Spirit transacts the process of our spiritual adoption, bringing us into the new family of God. The Spirit rescues us from being spiritual orphans, establishing and confirming us as true sons and daughters of the Heavenly Father!

All of this is made possible by what Jesus accomplished for us on the cross. Through His death and resurrection we are redeemed and forgiven, justified, and declared righteous. He paid the price for our freedom from sin and slavery and gave us a new identity as adopted daughters or sons of the Father.

The Father sent His Son so we might receive the legal status of adoption, but He sent the Holy Spirit so we might receive the emotional experience of

> OUR SALVATION STATUS HELPS US *KNOW* WE BELONG, BUT THE HOLY SPIRIT HELPS US *FEEL* LIKE WE BELONG.

adoption. Our salvation status helps us *know* we belong, but the Holy Spirit helps us *feel* like we belong.

4. The Abba Father cry. The ground is now set for the Holy Spirit to release in us the Abba Father cry: *"And by him we cry, 'Abba, Father'"* (Romans 8:15).

Let me repeat: the Abba Father cry that God wants for us is produced by the Holy Spirit; it is not of our own making. In John's gospel, Jesus says, *"Flesh gives birth to flesh, but the Spirit gives birth to spirit"* (John 3:6).

There is a fatherly cry we can produce out of our own intention and effort, but it is not the same as a Spirit-produced cry. This human cry is limited and short-lived, and ultimately prevents us from fully connecting with the Father. Any effort to generate affection for our Heavenly Father on our own is just another attempt to attain spiritual results by human effort. This never works.

The Abba Father cry that genuinely connects us with the love of the Father is produced within us by the Holy Spirit. This cry is both a receiving and giving of His love, a two-way exchange of love between the Heavenly Father and His child. The Holy Spirit makes it all possible, originating from One who has always dwelt with the Father in a place of belonging, worship, and adoration. We are invited to join our hearts with the Holy Spirit, who is always crying out "Abba, Father."

This cry has existed from eternity past and is granted to you and me as we come into our truest identity as God's beloved children. We are now able to cry out "Abba, Father, Daddy" and connect with God the Father in this profoundly close and personal way. We can begin to truly feel the love and affection of our adoptive Heavenly Father as we cry out to Him with love and affection from our hearts.

In Romans, Paul describes this Spirit-led process: *"God's love has been poured out into our hearts through the Holy Spirit, who has been given to us"* (Romans 5:5). The work of the Holy Spirit is to pour out the Father's love into our hearts. Sometimes we receive God's love like a steady drip, and other times it's like a drenching downpour. People experience both ends of this spectrum in different seasons of their lives, but however God's love is given, it is the work of the Spirit to pour the Father's love into our hearts.

5. The Spirit testifies. Finally, we arrive at a moment of testimony: *"The Spirit himself testifies with our spirit that we are God's children"* (Romans 8:16).

This important truth is sometimes overlooked. We must understand what it means that the Holy Spirit testifies with our spirit about our status as God's child. The word testify means "to bear witness, to provide supporting evidence by means of a testimony."[7]

So what exactly does the Spirit testify with our spirit? For one, He testifies to us what He hears the Father say about us. The Holy Spirit tells us that we are loved and a delight to the Father, that He is well pleased with us and enjoys our companionship. The Spirit also testifies that we matter to God, that He notices us, and that we are important to Him. No detail of our lives goes unnoticed by Him.

We need to hear the Spirit testify deeply to our spirits that we are God's children—that we belong, are loved, accepted, and valued. This is a profound and life-changing Spirit-to-spirit revelation.

The Spirit also speaks to our spirits about who the Father is and what He is like. The Spirit brings honour and glory to the Father, which is part of the Abba Father cry. He is constantly praising the Father and invites us to join Him in that expression of worship. The Spirit says things like "You are worthy, Father. Worthy of all praise, honour and glory. There is no one like You… majestic, powerful, sovereign, righteous, the only true God. I love You, Father." That's the Abba Father cry the Father longs to hear from our hearts.

The Holy Spirit tells us that everything the Father has is ours through Christ. We get to share in His heavenly inheritance. We are given access to all the Father has, all His heavenly riches and resources: *"Now if we are children, then*

---

7   William Arndt, et al, *A Greek-English Lexicon of the New Testament and Other Early Christian Literature* (Chicago, IL: Chicago Press, 2001), 957.

we are heirs—heirs of God and co-heirs with Christ, if indeed we share in his sufferings in order that we may also share in his glory"(Romans 8:17).

Able to Hear

To receive this revelation from the Spirit, we must become still enough to listen. We won't hear the Spirit's deep testimony when our spirits are distracted. This is central to experiencing the Father's love. It depends on our ability to hear and receive what the Spirit is saying to us.

As such, we must prepare our hearts. We must learn to quiet our minds and wait in His presence. We need to learn to slow down in our spirits and become still.

Years ago, the Spirit highlighted a section from the words of John the Baptist to me: *"The friend who attends the bridegroom waits and listens for him, and is full of joy when he hears the bridegroom's voice"*(John 3:29). This is exactly what it means to become aware of God's presence and hear the Spirit reveal the loving voice of the Father to us.

The transaction in John's words is simple: wait, listen, and then hear—and experience joy! But learning to be quiet and still enough to really hear God's voice is difficult in the context of the loud and distracting world in which we live. Great intentionality and practice is required to become still and know the present reality of God (Psalm 46:10).

I have learned to quiet myself in God's presence by taking intentional time in an undistracted environment to be alone with Him. For me, first thing in the morning works best. I simply sit still for a few moments, breathing slowly, focusing my thoughts on God, and telling Him how wonderful He is and how much I love Him. Using simple words of praise, I thank Him for His peace, presence, and goodness. I offer my whole person to Him as a living sacrifice—body, soul, and spirit. Sometimes I will lay facedown before Him, with my arms outstretched as a symbolic act of surrender. I ask Him to settle my busy mind and distracted spirit with His presence and love. Then I spend time reading the Bible. In doing this, I find my soul becoming quiet and God's presence becoming tangible and His voice audible.

This is how I, as a child of the Father, wait and listen for Him, and when I hear the Father's voice, I am filled with joy!

Take some time right now to think how this might look for you. Each of us is created with a different way of connecting with God. How do you best quiet your soul? It may be taking a walk outdoors in God's beautiful creation. It may be listening to God-honouring music and worshiping. It may be praying while you're driving. Even if your life is busy and overcrowded, think of ways you can find a few moments to be still, wait, and listen for the Father's voice.

The Spirit invites you to join Him in crying out, "Abba Father." Stop trying to produce this on your own and surrender to the work of the Holy Spirit. Begin to pray "Abba, Father, Daddy" to your Heavenly Father, and experience this cry welling up from deep within you as you join the Holy Spirit's heart with yours.

Read Romans 8:14–17 again and again, turning each sentence into a prayer. Pray those words right now: "Abba, Father, I love You. You are my Father. Thank You, praise You, Father God." Let the Spirit birth the Abba Father cry in your spirit. The more you pray into this cry, the more it will grow within you.

The Judge and the Criminal

Here's a story that helps illustrate the concept of spiritual adoption.

I am led into a courtroom.

"All rise!" the bailiff calls as the judge enters and takes his seat of authority.

The judge addresses me: "You are charged with a crime deserving the death penalty. How do you plead?"

I realize that I defiantly broke the law and, try as I might to deny it, the truth is that I am guilty and there's plenty of evidence to prove it. I think back over my whole life and painfully recall the choices I made.

This realization feels like a crushing hundred-pound weight on my shoulders. For the first time in my life, I give up my attempts to justify my evil actions and finally admit the truth. I surrender to the inevitable.

"Guilty, your honour," I say. "I plead guilty to the crime."

The judge, holding absolute authority over me, stares at me for a long moment. I see a strange glimpse of familiarity in his face.

The silence is finally broken when he says, "Based on the evidence against you and your own admission of guilt, I have no choice but to sentence you to the death penalty—the just and righteous punishment for the crime you have committed."

My heart sinks. This comes as no surprise, yet the reality strikes me afresh. It's hard for me to remain standing.

Suddenly, just as the judge lifts his gavel to seal my fate, a young man walks into the courtroom. I faintly recognize him as a person I knew in my childhood, but I haven't seen him in many years.

The young man walks right up to the judge's bench and, to my surprise, addresses him.

"Father, I want to take this man's place and receive the punishment he deserves," the man says.

This is the judge's son! I am paralyzed in confusion.

The judge himself looks surprised. "Son, there is no precedent for this. This matter does not involve you. Why should you make such a request?"

"Because I know this person," the son replies. "We used to be friends and I want him to be set free, to have a chance at a new life."

Friends? I stare at the young man, racking my brain, trying to remember what he and I may have shared in the past that would establish such a sense of connection. I don't have a recollection of being a good friend with anyone, let alone the kind of friend who would deserve such an intervention.

The judge speaks. "Son, do you understand that the crimes committed are punishable by death? You are innocent and have committed no crime."

"Father," the son says, "my love for my guilty friend is what compels me to offer my life in his place."

The judge seems stunned. There is a prolonged silence as the two, father and son, stare at each other in a painful, wordless exchange.

I and the others in the courtroom are frozen in silence. In this moment, we are all bystanders, witnesses to an unimaginable decision.

After what seems like an eternity, the judge turns away from his son and looks at me. "Your sentence is hereby transferred to this man, who is my son, and who has offered to serve your sentence on your behalf. As such, all charges against you have been dropped. You are declared innocent and your record is cleared of wrongdoing. You are free to go."

The gavel hits the desk like a hammer pounding a nail.

My head spins and I need to sit down. I can't believe what has just taken place. This can't really be happening! No one has ever shown such kindness to me in my entire life. It makes no sense.

Is it true? Am I really free? Is my record clean? Have I really been forgiven? Can the judge actually do this?

As the shocked spectators leave the courtroom, the judge's son is handcuffed and led away.

The judge asks me to join him in his chambers. When we are alone, he says, "My son has lovingly and willingly made your freedom possible today. It breaks my heart to condemn him in your place, but he made this choice of his own free will."

I have nothing to say. I feel as though I've been tossed around in a whirlwind that is beyond my comprehension and control.

The judge and I sit in silence for a while.

"I do have one request of you," he says after a period of silence. "Would you come visit me at my house? Would you let me get to know you? Would you consider the possibility of one day living with me in my house? Even more, would you let me adopt you and make you my son? Would you become part of my family and take my name and let me love you as my own child?"

This is too much to for me take in. Being set free is one thing, but an offer like this? I feel so unworthy and undeserving. I'm a criminal deserving death and here is this kind and loving judge offering me a lifetime of love and security.

What should I do?

What would you do?

Dear reader, the Spirit answers this question by saying that we can trust this offer from the eternal Judge who wants to be our Father. It may be astonishing, unexpected, gracious, and undeserved, but it is real. This is a *hesed* story. The Father and Judge wants us to live with Him in His home and learn what it means to be a beloved child who can cry out, "Abba, Father, Daddy."

Abba, Father, Daddy, thank You for Your love for me. Thank You for adopting me as one of Your own. I love You, Father. I want to live like one of Your true children, experiencing a tender and personal love relationship with You.

Holy Spirit, increase the Abba Father cry within me. Show me what the Father is saying about me and how He feels about me. Help me have a child-like heart of pure love that brings great joy and honour to my Father.
In Jesus's name, amen.

Questions for Reflection

1. How do you understand the Abba Father cry? Have you ever experienced it? What does it sound like? What does it feel like?
2. What role does the Holy Spirit play in producing the Abba Father cry in our hearts according to Romans 8:15–16?
3. Review the process of developing the Abba Father cry that is presented in this chapter. Where are you at in the process?
4. Learning to be still and focused on God will help us cultivate the Abba Father cry in our hearts. What are some things that help you to quiet your spirit and wait in God's presence? How do you best connect with God?

PREPARING TO ENCOUNTER
THE FATHER'S LOVE

Chapter Eight

The Abba Father cry is a core longing of our hearts when we come into a relationship with the Heavenly Father through Jesus Christ. An experience of His love is unique and personal to each of us. There is no prescribed way of initiating and creating this encounter. It's produced by the Holy Spirit, who moves in His own way and time.

This does not mean, however, that we are to sit passively, waiting for God to do what He will. Even though it's a work of the Holy Spirit, we have a role in making ourselves available for an encounter with the Father's love. The question is, what can we do to make ourselves open and receptive to the love of our Abba Father?

Here are several practical things we can do to help us experience the Heavenly Father's heart of love for us.

I. Be hungry. One of the most important qualities that will draw you towards God is a posture of desire and hunger. We must desire His love, desperately long for it, and do whatever it takes to receive it.

Jesus speaks about this kind of hunger:

Which of you fathers, if your son asks for a fish, will give him a snake instead? Or if he asks for an egg, will give him a scorpion? If you then, though you are evil, know how to give good gifts to your children, how much more will your Father in heaven give the Holy Spirit to those who ask him!

—Luke 11:11–13

The child in Jesus's teaching is hungry. He is asking for food. The child makes his request based on faith in the goodness of his father's heart, whom he knows is willing and able to grant his request. This is clearly a father who loves to give good gifts and doesn't ignore the hungry cry of his child.

Like the child in Jesus's story, do we hunger for a taste of the Father's love and goodness? Jesus makes a profound promise to those who come to the Father with a similar posture as the child in the story: *"how much more will your Father in heaven give the Holy Spirit to those who ask him!"* (Luke 11:13). How much more! That phrase says it all: there is always more that God wants to give you. An abundance of gifts is generously given through the outpouring of His Holy Spirit.

> HE IS A GOD OF
> MORE, SO DON'T
> SETTLE FOR LESS.

He is a God of more, so don't settle for less. Don't settle for just a small experience of His love; ask Him for more. He loves to give us more than what we can ask for or even imagine (Ephesians 3:20).

Are we hungry for His love in our lives?

Hunger compels us to cry out to Him for an outpouring of His love with child-like urgency and faith. Hunger drives our desire beyond simply seeking God's gifts to seeking God Himself—His presence and love.

Author and speaker Rob Reimer states it well: "We are to seek God's face and not just His hands. Seek God for intimacy with Him and not just for what He can do for us."[8]

2. Be shamelessly audacious. As we assume this posture of hunger, we are invited to a level of boldness that may be unfamiliar to many. Jesus describes this level of intensity in His story of a person in need asking a friend for help:

> *Then Jesus said to them, "Suppose you have a friend, and you go to him at midnight and say, 'Friend, lend me three loaves of bread; a friend of mine on a journey has come to me, and I have no food to offer him.' And suppose the one inside answers, 'Don't bother me. The door is already locked, and my children and I are in bed. I can't get up and give you anything.' I tell you, even though he*

---

8   Rob Reimer, *Deep Faith: Developing Faith that Releases the Power of God* (Franklin, TN: Carpenter's Son Publishing, 2017), 73.

will not get up and give you the bread because of friendship, yet because of your
shameless audacity he will surely get up and give you as much as you need."

—Luke 11:5–8

The Greek word *anaideia*, translated in the New International Version as "shameless audacity," means a "lack of sensitivity to what is proper, carelessness about the good opinion of others, shamelessness, impertinence, impudence, ignoring of convention."[9] This, and nothing less, is the posture that Jesus invites us to take.

This shameless audacity stands in contrast to what many church cultures practice and model: namely, restraint and hesitancy to let our hearts feel something for God. I'm not advocating for wild, free-for-all gatherings, but rather freedom from being bound by manmade traditions that repress the hearts of sincere followers of Jesus.

In Jesus's story in Luke 11:5–8, there is a real sense of urgency and desperation in the way this person asks his friend for help. Many of us are reluctant to be urgent and desperate in the way we pray to God. We think it's improper to beg God for help in our time of need, when in fact, like the person in the story, God will find this intense and shameless seeking of Him irresistible. God's heart is moved when we bring our desperate, needy, seeking hearts to Him. So we shouldn't hold back.

Recently the Lord brought my attention to this verse in Isaiah: *"For a long time I have kept silent, I have been quiet and held myself back. But now, like a woman in childbirth, I cry out, I gasp and pant"* (Isaiah 42:14). Now is the time for us to stop holding ourselves back from everything God has for us and cry out for more from the Lord.

3. Be cleansed. Having a clean life is another quality we must bring to God in order to experience His love. If we come to God with a life full of sin, crowded with love for the world, our experience of God's loving presence will be hindered. Our capacity for intimacy with God will be drastically reduced.

---

9   Walter F. Wilbur Bauter, et. al., *A Greek-English Lexicon of the New Testament and other early Christian Literature* (Chicago IL: University of Chicago Press, 1952), 63.

If we want to experience the love of the Father, we need our lives to be *"swept clean and put in order"* (Luke 11:25). Jesus speaks further about this need for cleansing later in Luke 11:

> *Your eye is the lamp of your body. When your eyes are healthy, your whole body also is full of light. But when they are unhealthy, your body also is full of darkness. See to it, then, that the light within you is not darkness. Therefore, if your whole body is full of light, and no part of it dark, it will be just as full of light as when a lamp shines its light on you.*
>
> —Luke 11:34–36

We need to be full of the Holy Spirit's presence so the powers of darkness have no legal ground to gain access in our lives. We have to get rid of the garbage so the rats have no place to feed. This involves a process of cleansing, which includes confessing our sin, repenting and renouncing that sin, receiving God's forgiveness, and then asking the Holy Spirit to fill our lives so there is no room for the powers of darkness.[10]

We aren't talking about perfection here. Sin and temptation are always present, attempting to draw us away from God. Rather, we are talking about receiving a clean heart and life through the cleansing blood of Christ and allowing His Spirit full access to our hearts. This is the way to pursue holiness and Christlikeness, and to experience the Heavenly Father's love.

4. Learn to live out of your heart. Too many wonderful Christians live primarily out of their heads and very little from their hearts. In our relationship with God, we must resist the cultural pull towards intellectual-only living. These are constructs of our Greek-influenced western culture, which if left unchecked can cause us to drift from a biblically balanced way of living.

The Bible has something very different to say than western culture dictates. In the New International Version, the word translated as heart in English is mentioned 725 times while the word translated as mind is mentioned 163 times. In the gospels, we see a similar ratio, with heart mentioned forty-nine times and mind referred to only seventeen times.

---

10 We will return to this subject in Chapter Ten.

According to the scriptures, the heart—referring to the centre of our emotional and feeling faculties—is the driving force of our lives, whether we like it or not. What fills our heart determines our behaviour far more than what fills our mind. This is why Proverbs says, *"Above all else, guard your heart, for everything you do flows from it"* (Proverbs 4:23).

We shouldn't be afraid to live out of our hearts. This is especially challenging for those of us who have experienced emotional wounds. There is a self-protective reflex that says, "I'm not going to allow myself to be emotionally vulnerable. I'll only get hurt again." In order to cross this gap, we need to allow God to heal our emotions so they can be expressed freely and appropriately.

I grew up in a dysfunctional home where strong, negative emotions were either expressed hurtfully or bottled up completely. I've been on a long journey learning to express strong emotions in a healthy and constructive way. I have a very patient wife who has helped me learn the language of emotions and how to express them fluently.

If we allow Him, God will lovingly bring healing to our emotions. Our heart is safe in the hands of our Heavenly Father; He will cherish it, protect it, and nurture it. He will also expand its capacity to love more and receive more of His love.

5. Be patient. Patience with God's timing is another quality we must bring to Him in order to experience His love. We can't demand anything from God. No relationship of love deals in the currency of demands.

Rather, our engagement with the Father deals in exchanges of *hesed*, made possible through the earnest and patient cultivation of intimacy. Hebrews 11:6 compels us to press in, by faith, to this patient process based on the belief that the Heavenly Father *"rewards those who earnestly seek him"* (Hebrews 11:6).

Some people give up on the opportunity to experience the Father's love because it never seems to come. They become discouraged by what feels, at times, like God's apparent lack of willingness to answer their prayers or make Himself known in the way they hope.

I can't explain God's timing. If you can relate to feeling impatient at times, I ask you to not give up, but to wait patiently for the Father to pour out His love for you. God knows best about what we need and when we need it. He really does reward those who earnestly seek Him.

6. Be receptive to prayer. Encountering God's love often requires the faith-filled prayers of fellow believers who themselves have had a deep experience of God's love. Find people who will pray for you and help you deal with any barriers to God's love in your life, and help you connect with the Father's heart.

The two things that most often prevent people from seeking prayer ministry from others are pride and fear. We have to repent of pride and push through our fears. Ask the Father to reveal what's holding you back from asking others for prayer. Then invite the Lord and His people to help you take steps to overcome those barriers.

The promise of James 5 speaks pointedly to the important ministry of the body of Christ to one another in prayer: *"Therefore confess your sins to each other and pray for each other so that you may be healed. The prayer of a righteous person is powerful and effective"* (James 5:16).

Here's the story of a friend who has experienced progressive healing with the help of God's people:

> Although I grew up in a Christian home, my life was full of pain and wounding. As a young child, I had been sexually abused. This gave way to fear that followed me for many years.
>
> As a teen, I experienced severe rejection that led to depression. I was so distressed that I tried to end my life, but my mother intervened and helped me to carry on. I eventually married a young man who I thought would bring me happiness, but life with him was full of abuse. Our marriage ended when he left me for another woman.
>
> I was devastated and wanted to end my life again, but in that moment of desperation I heard a voice say that my children needed me.
>
> Something shifted inside me as I found the courage to carry on. Over the years I have invited family and friends to pray for me and I sought out godly counselling. And while this certainly helped, I realized that more was needed.

So for a number of months I have been receiving comprehensive inner healing and deliverance ministry. God has been doing a deep work in me that has taken me through every stage of life with all its hurts and wounds.

I now feel held in the Father's arms as I find healing, forgiveness, freedom, and breakthrough. My depression has lifted and I no longer need the antidepressants I took for over twenty years! I am full of joy and peace, and fear is no longer my constant companion.

A friend I hadn't seen for months shared that she no longer sees fear written on my face. Father God has delivered me from the darkness and brought me into a place of light.

7. Be eager to give it away. When God gives us a good gift, He expects us not to hoard it, but to share it with others. Jesus calls us to live this way: *"Freely you have received; freely give"* (Matthew 10:8).

I've found that as I give away to others what God has given me, my capacity increases to receive even more from God. As you and I experience more of the Father's love, we will be able to share more of it with others. This is how the movement of the Father's love will grow and increase—from one person to another, sharing His love with everyone we can.

Even though receiving the Father's love is a Spirit-given gift, these postures and practices are some things we can do to prepare ourselves to receive. This is God's promise to us: *"Open wide your mouth and I will fill it"* (Psalm 81:10).

The Long Road of Love

We can't rely on dramatic, periodic experiences of God's love in order to know we're loved by God. We need to learn a consistent walk of attentiveness to the Father and receive His love every day in quiet and gentle ways.

It's possible to live every day feeling loved by God through the normal routine of life. We must learn to live in constant availability to God, openness to His Spirit, and attentiveness to His voice.

The daily spiritual disciplines of reading scripture, praying, worshipping, journaling, obeying, and serving are just some of the ways that help us stay in a place of experiencing His love. The added practices of fasting, silence, solitude, and sabbath rest will only increase our growing connection to the heart of the Father.

Surprised by God

Let me address the widely held belief that the Father expresses His love to us only in ways to which we can relate. In other words, if I am intellectually oriented, I will only connect intellectually with His love. If I am heart-oriented, I will only connect with His love emotionally.

While this can often be true, we must not slip into a belief that limits our experience of God by setting the terms for how the Father connects with us. Too many people are stuck in a mindset in which they dictate the way God must express His love to them. Most would deny that they're doing this, but it's the natural result when someone has decided in advance how God will move and work.

Prepare to be surprised by God. Be open to an unexpected encounter with the Father. God loves to surprise His people. Just when we think we have God figured out and can predict exactly what He'll do, He does something totally unexpected. God will not be controlled. I urge you to be open to the Father pouring out His love for you in a way you have never before experienced.

There are a number of biblical examples of people encountering God's presence in surprising ways. Israel's first king, Saul, met God in an unexpected way in I Samuel 10. After being anointed by Samuel, he met a procession of prophets:

> . . .the Spirit of God came powerfully upon him, and he joined in their prophesying. When all those who had formerly known him saw him prophesying with the prophets, they asked each other, "What is this that has happened to the son of Kish? Is Saul also among the prophets?"
>
> —I Samuel 10:10–11

It was a change so surprising that those who knew Saul couldn't believe what they were seeing.

In the New Testament, another Saul, who became the apostle Paul, had a surprising encounter with God's presence. One day, while on the way to

Damascus to carry out his anti-Christian crusade as a Pharisee and persecutor of the early church, Saul met God in a way that was both terrifying and life-altering:

> *As he neared Damascus on his journey, suddenly a light from heaven flashed around him. He fell to the ground and heard a voice say to him, "Saul, Saul, why do you persecute me?"*
>
> —Acts 9:3–4

Saul was temporarily blinded by the powerful presence of God, but then his eyes were opened to truly see God for the first time in his life. As a result he became one of the greatest apostles and missionaries of the New Testament.

A Story of Surprise

A friend of mine was once greatly surprised by the Father's love for him. This young man has a brilliant mind and works in the world of finance as a managing director with a big fund management company. His degrees are in finance and math, having obtained nearly a perfect GPA. He is a Chartered Financial Analyst, was valedictorian of his graduating class, and the recipient of a prestigious academic medal. He has managed one of the world's largest pension funds, a portfolio of $2.5 billion. He was the youngest fund manager in the company's history!

He is also a person with a genuine faith in Christ. But as you might suspect, he lived mostly out of his head when it came to relating to the Father. He could be described as an achiever for God, performance-oriented in the way he lived out his faith.

He was on a castle tour in northern England when he found himself alone on a beautiful beach. He observed some children happily playing and felt the warmth of a child's simple joy.

Then he heard some words and thoughts in his spirit that were not his own. The Voice was instantly recognizable, but the intimacy of the words was new.

"You are defined by who you are," the Father spoke directly to him. "Not by what you do or what you've accomplished, but by being you. You are a child of God, an innocent kid playing at the Father's feet. Nothing more. That is eternity... days without doing. Real sabbath days, being in the moment, not being measured or judged."

Hearing these words from the Father and experiencing His love came as a complete surprise. He couldn't remember a time in his life when the Father had spoken to him in such a personal and profound way.

That experience on the beach has had a lasting impact on the way he relates to His Heavenly Father. He now experiences the Father's love in his heart, not only in his mind. Even though he knows he has a long way to go on his journey, he is forever grateful that the Father surprised him with this gift of love.

Dear reader, if you have a tendency to prewrite the script of how God will work in your life, please ask yourself why. Is it due to fear? The need to be in control? An unwillingness to change? God will never do anything to harm you. All His ways are good and loving, but sometimes He helps us grow and change by stretching us in unexpected and surprising ways.

Let's pray this prayer now:

Father, I'm hungry for Your love. Please fill me as I open my heart wide to receive. Increase the intensity of my desire for You. I believe You are a Father who gives good gifts to Your children, and will give much more than I can even ask or imagine. Father, I am waiting and ready for You to pour out Your love for me. Thank You!
In Jesus's name, amen.

Questions for Reflection

1. This chapter presents several practical ways in which we can prepare ourselves to connect with the Father's heart of love for us. Which of these ways stand out to you the most and why?
2. What steps do you need to take in order to implement these preparatory postures in your life?
3. How hungry are you for the Father's love?

Is Feeling God's Love Really Necessary?

Chapter Nine

Is feeling God's love really necessary? This is a key question for many people who wonder why it isn't enough to simply know that God loves us. Why do we need to experience God's love? What does this even mean? Doesn't the experience create a new and subjective standard by which to measure God's love for us? How do you measure an experience? Isn't there a more objective way to know that God loves us? If a person doesn't feel God's love, does that mean they're lacking something in their life?

These are valid and important questions!

The answer to the question of the necessity of feeling God's love is both yes and no. Yes, experiencing the Father's love is necessary for enjoying an abundant life, but it's not necessary for eternal life. Feeling His love isn't one of the marks of being a true Christian; it's not the basis of our faith or the reason to serve and obey Him.

The truth, however, is that God desires for us to feel His love! It is, in fact, a crucial component of the abundant life Jesus invites all of His disciples to experience: *"I have come that they may have life, and have it to the full"* (John 10:10).

Human relationships that don't include a vital emotional connection are relegated to the realm of acquaintances—people we may know casually, but never those in whom we fully invest. We would not focus on giving and receiving care with them, or sharing deep thoughts and ideas, or deep emotions such as joy, grief, sorrow, and excitement.

What kind of relationship would we have with our Heavenly Father if we never experienced an emotional connection with Him? He is the One who created us and longs for us to experience His presence in our lives.

In the Garden of Eden, an active friendship existed between Adam and Eve and the Father. He was with them at all times. And when they were separated by sin, He called out, *"Where are you?"* (Genesis 3:9) He longed to restore their intimate friendship.

Sadly, many Christians go through life having an emotionless relationship with the Heavenly Father. They acknowledge their need for salvation, but after that God is more of an acquaintance for them. They engage with Him based solely on head knowledge, with little to no sense of emotional connection. Formality replaces familiarity; the relationship is functional, but they miss the full experience of having the abundant life the Father wants them to experience in Christ. God's love *for us* is meant to create love *in us*. When we know we're loved and forgiven, and feel loved and forgiven, we are able to live like His true sons and daughters.

With our earthly fathers, no emotional connection is required for a son or daughter to come into

> GOD'S LOVE *FOR US* IS MEANT TO CREATE LOVE *IN US*.

being or carry on the lineage of the family. Most, however, would agree that the full benefit of fatherhood extends far beyond this. In a healthy parent/child relationship, the bond is known and felt, establishing the foundation for profound expressions of love, a flourishing sense of self-identity, and countless opportunities for joy in sharing life's journey together.

The Best Demonstration of the Father's Love

The Father's love is best understood and experienced through His Son, Jesus Christ, and ultimately exemplified through His death on the cross for us.

> *This is how we know what love is: Jesus Christ laid down his life for us. . .*
> *This is love: not that we loved God, but that he loved us and sent his Son as an atoning sacrifice for our sins.*
> —I John 3:16, 4:10

Jesus's death on the cross is the clearest and most profound demonstration of the fact that God loves you. This love from the Father compelled Him to make it possible for you to connect to His heart through His willingness to offer His Son to die for your sake. Jesus became the sacrifice for your sins, the only way for you to find forgiveness and be reconciled to the Heavenly Father. He longs for you to know Him here on earth and ultimately know Him fully in heaven.

Personally, it is beyond staggering to know that the Father chose me, an underserving sinner, with a love so strong that He brought me into a living relationship with Him through the redemptive work of His Son. How could the God of the universe love me so much that He would want to make me one of His own children?

I will never fully comprehend this good news of love. Knowing this results in a deep sense of being loved by God. Even after almost fifty years of knowing Him personally, thinking about this still stirs joy in my heart and brings tears to my eyes. I am His and He is mine, and nothing can separate us.

> *For I am convinced that neither death nor life, neither angels nor demons, neither the present nor the future, nor any powers, neither height nor depth, nor anything else in all creation, will be able to separate us from the love of God that is in Christ Jesus our Lord.*
>
> —Romans 8:38–39

A Story of Forgiveness

I love the story in Luke 7 of the sinful woman who intruded on a dinner at Simon the Pharisee's home to anoint Jesus's feet with expensive perfume. When the host saw this outrageous act, he was immediately offended that this sinful woman would do such a thing at a social gathering.

Knowing what was in Simon's heart, Jesus spoke these timeless and profound words: *"Therefore, I tell you, her many sins have been forgiven—as her great love has shown. But whoever has been forgiven little loves little"* (Luke 7:47). The obvious implication here is that whoever has been forgiven much, loves much!

I know how much I've been forgiven. Do you? The deep awareness of my sin and God's undeserved grace and forgiveness still moves me. It actually moves me more now that I'm older and have gotten to know my Heavenly Father better.

Even though I grew up in the church and knew about God, I became a prodigal son at sixteen years of age. I immersed myself in the world of girls, cars, and parties, pursuing these interests with a vengeance. I was looking for fulfillment and happiness, but ultimately found myself more miserable and frustrated.

But behind the scenes, God faithfully pursued me with His sovereign, persistent love.

I loved playing bass guitar and was invited to be part of a Christian musical group that played at a number of church services across the city. The only catch was that I had to sit and listen to a number of sermons!

God spoke to me very personally and clearly during those sermons. I felt a deep conviction from the Holy Spirit about my sinful choices and running away from God, turning my back on His love and kindness. I knew He was calling me to back to Him.

God's persistent love eventually brought me to my senses. After months of resisting God's invitation to return to Him, I attended a weekend youth retreat at a Christian camp—and there, with much relief and joy, I finally surrendered my life to Jesus and experienced the filling of the Holy Spirit.

I'll never forget that night. On Sunday, March 3, 1974 at 2:30 a.m., I had a dramatic experience of God's forgiveness and love. It felt like a hundred-pound weight being lifted off my back. I was filled with inexpressible joy and wanted to wake up the entire camp and tell them my good news!

Thankfully I had a level-headed roommate who suggested I wait until later that morning.

The next day when I opened the Bible, the words came alive! I wasn't just reading words on a page anymore; I was hearing God's voice in new ways. I had never experienced anything like this before. I was a truly changed person.

Some weeks later, I was asked to give a testimony of my new life in Christ, and despite my extreme nervousness, as I began to share, I sensed the Holy Spirit speaking through me. I was so surprised as the words flowed out of my mouth. All I had to do was keep talking and He gave me the words! This was my first taste of the gift of preaching and teaching.

My dramatic conversion and filling of the Spirit led to two of the greatest gifts I have ever been given: my call to pastoral ministry and my friendship with Audrey.

The first thing I did after the retreat on Monday morning was find Audrey at her school locker and tell her what had happened. I knew she would be delighted because she was already a strong, devoted Christian. She was overjoyed to hear my good news and we began a friendship which grew into a ministry partnership, which then grew into a romance, finally leading to marriage. I cannot be more thankful for Audrey and the way God brought us together. She is a true gift from God and the person He chose for me as my partner in marriage, family, and ministry for more than forty-three years—and counting.

I am so grateful to God for all His blessings. I don't deserve any of them. All I deserve from Him is punishment and eternal separation. But in His great love, He forgave my sins, which were many, and gave me the gift of His *hesed* love and eternal life.

God, from whom I deserve nothing, has given me everything. And if that wasn't enough, He called me to be a pastor and has faithfully carried me through five decades of service in His church. I will continue to serve Him with my whole being until my last breath.

Knowing that we are loved and forgiven in this way should move our hearts in a loving response toward our Heavenly Father. Knowing the extent of the Father's love for us should stir in us some kind of emotional expression. How can we not experience a heartfelt response of love for our Father who loves us with such an amazing love? There is no way to contain the grateful love we willingly offer back to God based on what He has done for us.

Feeling loved *by* God, and love *for* God, is necessary for a healthy love relationship with Him. When it comes to the expression of feelings, any one-sided love relationship is unhealthy. Conversely, a healthy relationship with God is a result of a mutual love relationship between the Father and His child.

Experiencing love for God isn't all about us, as though our experience is the central focus. The ultimate goal is to bring joy and honour to His name. The focus is on Him. We need to remember that the Father is the One who found us and rescued us, the One who we want to glorify forever. Our love for Him is a gift of worship that brings Him delight.

The point is for us to honour and please God with our lives—to bring joy to His heart by responding to His love for us. Just like any father whose heart is delighted when his child gladly receives and responds to his love for them, so the heart of our Heavenly Father is delighted with this mutual exchange of love with His children.

As we read in 1 John 4:19, *"We love because he first loved us."* God is the initiator and we're the responder; both of us receive and give love.

To be sure, each person will experience the love of the Father in unique and different ways. There is no one right way to feel loved by God. This is because each of us is fearfully and wonderfully made, having a unique personality, emotional makeup, and history that has shaped us into who we are. But God's love can touch us all in a way that is real, meaningful, and remarkable.

Dear reader, this is an experience worth having—a great gift that too many of us miss. Do we really need to feel God's love? Yes, we do! Let's talk to Him about that now:

> *Father, thank You for loving me and showing Your love by sending Your Son Jesus to die for me on the cross. I don't want to go through life unmoved by this most amazing gift of love. Open my heart to feel love for You in response to Your love for me.*
>
> *I want to be like a child responding to a wonderful, generous Father who has given me the best gift I could ever imagine. I open my heart now to know You, honour You, hear Your voice, and experience the depths of Your love for me. In Jesus's name, amen!*

Questions for Reflection

1. How convinced are you that feeling God's love is really necessary? Why or why not?
2. Bob tells the personal story of how the deep awareness of his sin and God's undeserved grace and forgiveness still moves him emotionally, producing a growing love for the Father. What part of his story can you relate to? How and why?
3. How is Jesus's death on the cross the clearest and most profound demonstration of the fact that God the Father loves you?

WHY CAN'T I FEEL
THE FATHER'S LOVE?

Chapter Ten

At this point, you might be asking, "Why can't I feel the Heavenly Father's love like this book suggests, or like other people do?" There are some definite reasons why people may have trouble connecting with the Father's heart of love.

Let's start with a story.

I don't have many dreams from the Lord, but when I do they're memorable and obvious. Some time ago, I dreamed I was in a house, standing in a hallway with doors leading to several rooms.

At the end of the hallway was a room with a closed door. The Lord showed me that this house, with all its rooms, was my life. Beyond that door at the end of the hallway was a secret room, a place where I kept things sealed off just for myself.

I'm not proud of the fact that I have a history of wanting to keep some things hidden, secretly and privately, behind a closed door.

In my dream, I walked to that door and opened it. Before me was a dark and stuffy room containing objects that didn't belong there. I turned on the light and opened the window to let in some fresh air. Then I cleaned out those items that didn't belong.

The Lord told me that I was to keep all the rooms of my life open and full of light—no secrets, no hidden places, no darkness, no shutting myself off from Him or other people. He reminded me of what the apostle John wrote: *"But if we walk in the light, as he is in the light, we have fellowship with one another, and the blood of Jesus, his Son, purifies us from all sin"* (I John 1:7).

I believe my dream points to one of the reasons many people cannot experience the Father's love for them. They have closed doors in their lives—barriers, obstacles, secrets, hidden things—that prevent them from freely receiving God's love. God wants us to open the door to these rooms and allow the light of His presence to shine in. He wants to partner with us to expose the hidden things, cooperate with Him to clean out these rooms, and let His love and light fill those spaces. God is ready, willing, and able to help us enter into this process.

In my experience, here are some common obstacles people need to address with God's help.

I. Sin, guilt, and shame. Behind that closed door may be sin that produces guilt and shame. If you find it hard to feel God's love for you, this is the most obvious starting place.

Getting rid of guilt and shame is as simple—but not always easy—as confessing the sin that causes it. You need to repent from the sin, renounce it in Jesus's name, and receive God's mercy and forgiveness.

When we accept God's forgiveness for sin, the guilt and shame will disappear and we'll be able to come out of hiding. We'll feel His love flow fully and freely once again into our lives.

> *If we confess our sins, he is faithful and just and will forgive us our sins and purify us from all unrighteousness.*
> —I John I:9

2. A distracted heart. Behind that closed door may be a room filled with many distractions, crowding out your awareness of the presence and love of God in your life. You may be full of love for many other things, even good things, but as a result, love for God is being displaced. A heart that is filled with the things of this world has a reduced capacity for experiencing the fullness of God's love.

> *Do not love the world or anything in the world. If anyone loves the world, love for the Father is not in them.*
> —I John 2:15

In Jesus's parable of the sower in Mark 4, the four types of soil are illustrations of people's receptivity to the things of God. I believe the most common type of soil among believers today is the thorny soil. Jesus explained it like this:

> *Other seed fell among thorns, which grew up and choked the plants, so that they did not bear grain. . . Still others, like seed sown among thorns, hear the word; but the worries of this life, the deceitfulness of wealth and the desires for other things come in and choke the word, making it unfruitful.*
> —Mark 4:7, 18–19

Sometimes the busyness of our lives chokes out the life of faith within us, rendering us unable to bear spiritual fruit. We need to remove these thorns and prepare the soil of our heart so that it is healthy and receptive to God and His love for us once again.

What are the distractions that are choking out the spiritual vitality in your life? What might you need to let go or get rid of that is distracting you or stretching you in too many directions?

The Bible calls us to be wholehearted, not half-hearted or divided in our heart. God's love flows in a heart that is fully devoted to Him. The Lord promises, *"You will seek me and find me when you seek me with all your heart"* (Jeremiah 29:13).

3. Wounds from the past. Behind that closed door might be a room filled with wounds from the past which need to be brought into the open and healed.

Often our mostly deeply rooted wounds, the most influential wounds in our lives, stem from our childhood. In discerning these blockages, it is imperative that we ask the Holy Spirit to show us where and how we've been hurt—whether it be by our parents, other family members, or anyone else.

When the Spirit points out such a wound, it must be dealt with, especially in the case of wounds inflicted by one's earthly father or mother. Often the help of a counsellor, or prayer with a trusted friend, is helpful in this process. When we honestly deal with these issues, we will be free to draw near to the Heavenly Father and experience His love.

4. The lies we believe. Behind that closed door may be lies about God, yourself, and others. These lies tell you that you're unworthy and unlovable. Or they say that God doesn't care about you, or that He won't give you the gifts

He gives to other people. Perhaps you believe that you'll never feel God's love and that you weren't meant to. Some people believe the lie that emotions are dangerous, that you're only a thinking person, not a feeling person.

We all believe lies to some degree. What are the lies you believe? Ask the Holy Spirit to show you these lies and address them directly with truth from the scriptures.[11]

Once you can identify the lies and discern the truth that can replace them, it's a matter of declaring truth over the lies in Jesus's name and beginning to live out of the truth.

5. Ungodly inner vows. Behind that closed door may be some ungodly inner vows we have made—promises to ourselves like "I will never be like my father/mother. I will never let myself be hurt again. I wish I had never been born. I wish I'd been born into a different family. I wish I was invisible."

A negative, ungodly vow built upon wounds and lies has the potential to become a spiritual declaration which gives power to the spirits of darkness. If not recognized, renounced, and broken, these ungodly inner vows can lead to strongholds of fear, hatred, bitterness, rebellion, and sometimes demonic oppression.

Ungodly vows can, and must be, broken through the cross of Jesus Christ and by the power of His blood. You can reverse the power of an ungodly vow by repentance and renunciation, then by blessing the person who is the object of your vow.[12]

6. Pride. Behind a closed door may be a room filled with the stuffiness of pride. I've met too many Christians who take the posture that they're "just fine." They've come as far as they need to, are satisfied in their relationship with the Lord, and see no need to grow further or deeper.

Pride is at the root of this mindset. God says that He is opposed to the proud (James 4:6), which means He cannot pour out a deep experience of His love into a proud heart.

---

11 Read more about dealing with lies in Chapter Twelve.
12 A list of helpful books that teach about this topic can be found in the bibliography at the end of this book.

These people have the mindset of the Pharisee in Luke's gospel who prayed, *"God, I thank you that I am not like other people—robbers, evildoers, adulterers—or even like this tax collector"* (Luke 18:11). In other words, they place themselves over and above others, saying "I am better than those people."

Sadly, there is so much judgment and criticism among God's people towards others today. This has become a cancer in the body of Christ, a false representation of Jesus which grieves the heart of the Father.

The Lord wants us to have the humble mindset of the tax collector in the same story who, in contrast to the Pharisee, simply prayed, *"God, have mercy on me, a sinner"* (Luke 18:13). In other words, "I need You, Lord. I'm desperate for Your mercy and grace. Apart from You, I am nothing. I've got a long way to go."

Pride runs deep in the human heart and is difficult to deal with. But the Father can demolish the stronghold of pride and help us develop true humility in our hearts. All that is needed on our part is genuine repentance and the willingness to embrace a *"broken and contrite heart"* (Psalm 51:17).

7. Unforgiveness. If you're withholding forgiveness from anyone, you're keeping the door to that room closed to God and the experience of His love. Unforgiveness is the most common barrier that prevents us from experiencing the Father's love and finding healing either physically, emotionally, or spiritually.

> UNFORGIVENESS IS THE MOST COMMON BARRIER THAT PREVENTS US FROM EXPERIENCING THE FATHER'S LOVE AND FINDING HEALING.

My oldest brother's story of forgiveness is one of my favourite examples. In Chapter One, I mentioned the terrible relationship my brother had with our dad. They were in constant conflict, including physical fights. As the oldest, my brother often took the brunt of my dad's alcohol-induced anger.

In the early 1970s, many years after our dad left, my brother experienced a period of renewal in his walk with God during a revival that was sweeping through western Canada. Many lives were being changed at this time. The Lord told my brother, "You have to forgive your dad. Your lack of forgiveness and bitterness toward him is blocking your relationship with Me. You can't grow any further spiritually until you forgive your father."

At first, my brother resisted this word from God. He thought our dad should be asking for *his* forgiveness, not the other way around! Then my brother realized that he had two choices: to keep going this way and remain spiritually stunted, or choose to forgive our dad and have a growing relationship with his Heavenly Father. My brother wrestled with this in his heart for quite a while until he could fight no longer.

He made the phone call to our dad.

My brother says it was the hardest call he ever had to make. He explained to Dad the reason he was calling and what the Lord wanted him to do. Then he told our dad that he forgave him. His exact words were, "I forgive you and am letting it go."

At the other end of the line, there was total silence. He hadn't heard Dad drop the phone and faint, so my brother assumed he must still be there, despite the long and awkward pause. Dad had no clue what he should say; he was completely taken by surprise and had no idea what to do with this unexpected offering of love and forgiveness (*hesed*).

To be sure, my brother hadn't expected him to say or do anything. The point was to just forgive him, no matter the outcome.

All Dad eventually said was "Okay."

After my brother hung up the phone, he said that he felt like an enormous weight had been lifted off his shoulders. He felt free from the years spent hating his father, and over the following months his relationship with God really took off. His sense of God's love for him changed. He had a new awareness of the great kindness and love the Heavenly Father had for him.

Later, he offered to meet with Dad and introduce him to his first grandchild. Dad accepted, and during the day they spent together he sincerely thanked my brother for the phone call.

But the story doesn't end there.

That first visit opened the door for me and my other two brothers to begin visiting our dad. I weep when I think about how the Lord showed my dad such undeserved love and grace, having his sons, whom he had abandoned, come see him and connect with him. It's truly a *hesed* story—when the one from whom you deserve nothing gives you everything.

For the remainder of my dad's life, Audrey and I enjoyed several visits and some great conversations. We shared not only our lives but also the gospel of Jesus Christ. I'm always amazed at the kind of doors that open when we obey the Lord and do what He says, even if it means the hard work of forgiving a person who doesn't deserve it.

If you can't feel the Father's love for you, it may be unforgiveness that's blocking the way.

8. Demonic oppression. Behind that closed door may be a room that's shrouded in the shadows of demonic oppression. Satan will do everything he can to block you from God's love. He has a range of tactics, the most common being accusation and condemnation. He will remind you of all your sins, faults, and failures and try to keep you locked in that room at the end of the hallway in a dark cycle of judgment, self-condemnation, and unworthiness.

When we give Satan a foothold in our lives, whether through sin, unforgiveness, unresolved anger, or rebellion, demonic forces are given legal access to oppress and torment us, blocking our hearts from experiencing God's love. Demonic oppression is when dark forces of evil are permitted to affect us.

You may be wondering what the difference is between demonic oppression and possession. True Christians cannot be possessed (owned, mastered) by demons, but they can be oppressed (influenced, affected).[13]

With the authority Jesus has given us over the powers of darkness, we can be released from demonic oppression and set free to feel God's love and walk in victory.

At times, deliverance prayer ministry by gifted and seasoned intercessors may be required to address demonic issues. We don't need to deal with these things alone! If you think you might be suffering in the darkness of demonic oppression, be willing to ask others for help.

---

13 For more detailed teaching on this topic, see: Charles Kraft, *I Give You Authority* (Ada MI, Chosen Books, Baker Publishing Group, 2012), 31–35; and Rob Reimer, *Soul Care: Seven Transformational Principles for a Healthy Soul* (Franklin, TN: Carpenter's Son Publishing, 2016), 203-238.

9. An emotionally repressed culture. Behind that closed door may be a room filled with obstacles placed in our way through emotionally repressed environments. Too many sincere followers of Jesus have only known family and church environments that are cerebral and subdued, downplaying feelings and emotion. We are taught that emotions are dangerous and unreliable, or unbecoming in a respectful environment of worship; we've been conditioned to believe they are better kept under control.

The result of this belief is people with repressed emotions who train themselves to not feel anything when it comes to their relationship with God. While being overly emotional can be unbalanced and extreme, we need to strike a balance of healthy emotion and thoughtful response in our relationship to the Father. People in the Bible often expressed themselves in worship by declaring truth to God, but also with tears, joy, shouting, and dancing.

If you have been shaped by an emotionally repressive culture, I would suggest that you get to know people who are free and balanced in their emotional expression of love toward God. Be willing to step out of your comfort zone and learn to express your heart to Him in a way that honours Him and sets your heart free. A good place to begin is through Christ-honouring worship environments where both hearts and minds are engaged in expressing love for God.

I believe that worship is one of the keys to unlocking our hearts and releasing godly emotion that is pleasing to God. Worship is a matter of both the mind and the heart: *"God is spirit, and his worshipers must worship in the Spirit and in truth"* (John 4:24). Remember that worship isn't about yourself. Worship is about the Father, Son, and Holy Spirit. Worship will set your heart free to feel genuine, God-honouring emotions.

10. Stubborn individualism. Behind that closed door may be the belief that you don't need others in your life. Going it alone in the Christian life is a recipe for stunted and deformed growth. Being part of a vital Christian community is crucial for someone to grow in maturity and be able to fully experience the love of the Father.

Many spend their lives looking for the perfect church that will meet all their wants and needs. This is futile. Commit yourself to a local church community where you can love, serve, and contribute instead of making it all about yourself. Your needs will be met as you focus on others.

Remember that you'll never get everything you want or need from a church community—you weren't meant to. You were meant to get everything you need from your relationship with Christ. He alone meets all our genuine needs, providing opportunities for fulfillment and growth through being with other believers in the context of relationship.

Relationships in the church are often complicated, like many family relationships. But they are necessary. As challenging as they may be, God has called us to be part of a church family so we can grow, mature, and collectively bring glory to God.

Learning to relate to others who are different than you offers a great opportunity for character development and growth. Proverbs 27:17 says, *"As iron sharpens iron, so one person sharpens another."* There is a fresh longing in the church for an authentic community of people who are joined together in loving relationship.

The early Christian church was a close-knit community devoted to God and each other. In Acts 2, they key word is devoted: *"They devoted themselves to the apostles' teaching and to fellowship, to the breaking of bread and to prayer"* (Acts 2:42).

Belonging to a church community means so much more than attending a weekly service. We are called to do life together as a family of God. Together we serve and give, as well as receive love and share love with others.

If you've been hurt by church leaders, then as someone who has been a leader in the church for many years I want to sincerely say, "I'm sorry." As leaders, we have done hurtful things and haven't always acted in a Christ-like way. Sometimes we have wounded God's people and fallen far short of our mandate of biblical love.

Please, ask the Lord to help you forgive those leaders who have hurt you. I implore you, don't remain stuck in your hurt, anger, and bitterness. You'll only hurt yourself in the long run.[14]

Experiencing the fullness of the Father's love requires the community of God's people to seek God together. This is reflected in a phrase in the prayer of Paul asking God to reveal the immensity of His love:

> *And I pray that you, being rooted and established in love, may have power, together with all the Lord's holy people, to grasp how wide and long and high and deep is the love of Christ, and to know this love that surpasses knowledge—that you may be filled to the measure of all the fullness of God.*
> —Ephesians 3:17–19 (emphasis added)

Over the years I've done some competitive long-distance running. I've run three full marathons, a dozen half-marathons, and many shorter distances.

My first marathon took me over five hours to complete. For this first long race, I was physically and strategically unprepared. About halfway through the run, I found myself at the end of my endurance, but I was determined to finish. With ten or so miles to go, a young man ran up beside me and said, "Hi Pastor Bob, how are you doing?" I had never seen this person before and didn't even have the presence of mind to ask his name.

When this young man saw that I was struggling—a sorry sight indeed—he said to me, "Okay, see that lamp post? Let's run to that and then we'll walk." Which we did together.

Then after a few minutes of walking together, he said, "Okay, see that intersection? Let's run that far and then we'll walk again." Which we did together.

With his coaching, encouragement, and companionship, we crossed the finish line together. He could have finished with a much better time, but he chose to run with me at my slower pace. While the few remaining spectators

---

14 I'm writing this chapter during the COVID-19 pandemic with restrictions that have affected the whole world. Having attended church online for many months, we have lost much of the enriching community life that is so important to us. We can't foresee what church will look like once this pandemic eases, but it will likely look different. One thing can never be replaced, and that is person-to-person connection. Connecting deeply with people will always be at the heart of God's gathered community. Let us all commit to an even deeper sense of community as we move forward as His church.

cheered us on, I thanked this young man without whose help I would not have finished.

To this day, I still don't know who he was!

This, to me, is a picture of the church—a variety of people, from various backgrounds, in various stages of growth and maturity, with different strengths and weaknesses, united by a common love for Christ and each other, who are devoted to the mission of the Kingdom and helping each other get across the finish line. What a privilege to be a part of a local church family!

Dear reader, which of these obstacles to the Father's love are hindering you most? Please take the time right now to talk to God about these obstacles and ask Him to help you find a way forward. Let us *"throw off everything that hinders and the sin that so easily entangles"* (Hebrews 12:1) so we can grow stronger in the Father's love.

> *Father, I want to feel the love You have for me. I desire this with all my heart. Please show me the things that hinder me from fully experiencing Your love. And please help me to deal with any barriers to Your love. I want to be healed and set free so I can have a growing sense of Your heart of love for me. Help me live with all the doors in my life wide open and filled with Your holy light.*
> *In Jesus's name, amen.*

Questions for Reflection

1. Which of the obstacles listed in this chapter hinder you the most from feeling the Father's love?

2. Bob writes that unforgiveness is the biggest barrier to feeling God's love. How do you respond to that statement? Is there anyone in your life you need to forgive? Who? Why? How ready and willing are you to forgive them?

3. What distractions are choking out the spiritual vitality in your life? What might you need to let go or get rid of that distracts you or stretches you in too many directions?

4. What steps can you take to address these obstacles and find the freedom to feel the Father's love?

You Woke Me Up
To Tell Me That?!

Chapter Eleven

" C ongratulations, Mr. Carroll! You have another son!"
These words would fill most dads with joy at the birth of their child. But not in my father's case.

I came into the world in the middle of the night on July 3, 1956. My father drove my labouring mom to the hospital, but he didn't stay in the waiting room. Instead, after dropping her off, he returned home and went to bed.

In the early morning hours, the phone rang, waking up the household. The doctor was calling to tell my father the news.

I know about all this from my oldest brother, who was ten at the time. His clear memory from the night I was born is centred around this early morning conversation between my father and the doctor. He vividly remembers standing nearby when my groggy father answered the call.

"Congratulations, Mr. Carroll!" the doctor said. "You have another son!"

My dad's response was angry and bothered. "You woke me up in the middle of the night to tell me *that*?" Immediately he slammed the phone down and went back to bed.

Welcome to the world, Bob!

I didn't realize it at the time, but those angry words—"You woke me up in the middle of the night to tell me *that*?"—placed a spirit of rejection on me that has plagued me. If I displeased my own father by my arrival as a baby, how could I possibly hope to gain acceptance and love from him or others? Throughout my life, I have struggled to believe I am loved and acceptable, which has led me to strive to gain people's approval.

The power of a father in the formation or malformation of his child's self-concept cannot be overstated. I was scarred before I was an hour old!

Fast-forward to the spring of 2020.

During a time of extended fasting and prayer, the Lord woke me up one night at three o'clock. I heard Him say, "Bob, get up and go downstairs. I want to meet with you."

As I sat on the couch, I asked the Lord, "So why exactly are we here? Couldn't this have waited until six or seven o'clock?"

I think God enjoys my sense of humour.

In the living room in the middle of the night, I experienced what felt like wave after wave of God's love filling me to overflowing. He was pouring His love into my heart. I sobbed with joy as I received this beautiful gift, given in the quiet darkness of night, a gift of tangibly encountering the Father's heart of love for me.

During this rich and wonderful experience, the Father brought to my mind the story of my birth and my earthly father's response. As I again experienced this painful memory, the Lord spoke to me using the very same language that had always haunted me.

But here's what I heard my Heavenly Father say: "Bobby, I woke you up in the middle of the night to tell you *that* I love you. That I'm glad you were born. That I was so happy on the night you came into the world. That I looked forward to the beginning of the life I planned out for you."

Waves of love flowed from the Father's heart into mine as words that had once been a curse became words of profound blessing. The fragments of a son's broken identity were collected and made whole again through the healing love of a perfect Heavenly Father.

I wish I could describe the depth of healing I received from the Father that night. The encounter transformed me. I have tears in my eyes even now as I write these words.

This wasn't an isolated event. It's only one of several powerful encounters I have had over the years when the Father poured His love upon me. Each of these encounters have been another step in the healing journey for the wounds and brokenness I experienced at the hand of my father.

Turning Evil to Good

The Heavenly Father specializes in taking hurtful and evil things in people's lives and making them good and life-giving. He turns a place of destruction into a place of growth. He transforms curses into blessings, suffering into strength, and failure into victory—if we let Him.

The story of Joseph comes to mind.

Joseph was the eleventh son of twelve brothers. His father favoured him above his older siblings and this fostered jealousy and anger amongst the others. He was given dreams from the Lord and, in the excitement of his youth, he shared those dreams with his family. According to the dreams, some day he would be their leader.

When they listened to his dreams, his brothers resented him all the more. In their jealousy, they callously sold Joseph to Ishmaelite slave vendors. The hurt, pain, and betrayal Joseph experienced must have been unimaginable.

Joseph went on to spend years in captivity working as a slave in Egypt. He was unfairly imprisoned, but eventually, through a miraculous series of events, was released and promoted to a place of great authority by Pharaoh. Joseph didn't realize at the time that he would play a key role in the preservation of his people, the nation of Israel, saving them from starvation during a horrible famine.

That famine drove his brothers to travel out of their land and seek help in Egypt, ultimately bringing them face to face with the brother they had mercilessly sold into slavery decades earlier and whom they now thought was dead.

Joseph recognized them immediately, awakening the hurt, pain, and betrayal he had endured. But he noticed that the youngest brother, Benjamin, was not among them.

He provided his brothers with food, but required that they return with their youngest brother before they could receive more.

In a carefully calculated moment, Joseph finally revealed his identity to this group of once-conniving, now-fearful brothers. In this exchange, Joseph made a remarkable declaration. It's one of the most moving verses in scripture: *"You intended to harm me, but God intended it for good to accomplish what is now being done, the saving of many lives"* (Genesis 50:20).

This perspective, that God has the capacity and desire to take pain and evil and repurpose it for goodness and wholeness, demonstrates His heart of *hesed* love. He has the power to transform our deep hurts into great victories.

With the help of the Holy Spirit, we can see the sovereign hand of a good God in our suffering, receive healing, and move past our woundedness.

As I said at the beginning of this book, my father wound has become my life's message through the healing love of my Heavenly Father. Likewise, your greatest hurt can become your greatest

> YOUR GREATEST HURT CAN BECOME YOUR GREATEST TESTIMONY.

testimony if you allow God to heal, restore, and redeem your past suffering, sin, and failure. He will turn to good what was intended for evil.

Redeeming Our Suffering

Unless we allow God to redeem our suffering, we will remain stuck in defeat and bitterness. Our enemy, the devil, wants nothing more than for people to be bound by the hurts done to them and live out their lives with closed, wounded hearts, shut down and distant from God and others.

Much has been written on this topic, but I'll mention a few key points that I believe are crucial to understand as we consider our own suffering.

1. The Heavenly Father is not the author of pain, suffering, and evil. Rather, suffering comes as the result of the fall of humanity and the introduction of sin into the world (Genesis 3).

> *Therefore, just as sin entered the world through one man, and death through sin, and in this way death came to all people, because all sinned...*
> —Romans 5:12

2. Pain, suffering, and evil are to be expected. This is part of life in a fallen world.

Dear friends, do not be surprised at the fiery ordeal that has come on you to test you, as though something strange were happening to you.

—I Peter 4:12

3. Through Christ's redeeming death, pain and suffering can have a redemptive purpose. As we read in I Peter 1:6–7,

In all this you greatly rejoice, though now for a little while you may have had to suffer grief in all kinds of trials. These have come so that the proven genuineness of your faith—of greater worth than gold, which perishes even though refined by fire—may result in praise, glory and honor when Jesus Christ is revealed.

One redeeming purpose for our suffering may be that of discipline:

". . .the Lord disciplines the one he loves, and he chastens everyone he accepts as his son."
Endure hardship as discipline; God is treating you as his children. For what children are not disciplined by their father?

—Hebrews 12:6–7

Suffering can also lead to a refining of our character:

Not only so, but we also glory in our sufferings, because we know that suffering produces perseverance; perseverance, character; and character, hope.

—Romans 5:3–4

It can make us more Christ-like:

I want to know Christ—yes, to know the power of his resurrection and participation in his sufferings, becoming like him in his death. . .

—Philippians 3:10

Additionally, suffering can make us more caring of others and deepen our human relationships:

"...the God of all comfort, who comforts us in all our troubles, so that we can comfort those in any trouble with the comfort we ourselves receive from God."
—2 Corinthians 1:3–4

It can also point us to a restored heaven and earth in the future:

Now if we are children, then we are heirs—heirs of God and co-heirs with Christ, if indeed we share in his sufferings in order that we may also share in his glory.
I consider that our present sufferings are not worth comparing with the glory that will be revealed in us. 19 For the creation waits in eager expectation for the children of God to be revealed.
—Romans 8:17–19

And finally, it can create in us a longing for heaven:

I consider that our present sufferings are not worth comparing with the glory that will be revealed in us.
—Romans 8:18

But rejoice inasmuch as you participate in the sufferings of Christ, so that you may be overjoyed when his glory is revealed.
—1 Peter 4:13

4. God identifies with our pain and suffering. He became fully human in the person of Jesus Christ.

For we do not have a high priest who is unable to empathize with our weaknesses, but we have one who has been tempted in every way, just as we are—yet he did not sin.
—Hebrews 4:15

5. The day is coming when all suffering will end. Revelation 21:3–5 tells us,

And I heard a loud voice from the throne saying, "Look! God's dwelling place is now among the people, and he will dwell with them. They will be his people, and

God himself will be with them and be their God. 'He will wipe every tear from their eyes. There will be no more death' or mourning or crying or pain, for the old order of things has passed away."

He who was seated on the throne said, "I am making everything new!"

—Revelation 21:3–5

Suffering and pain are difficult to face, but don't bury your suffering, saying, "It's too painful. I'm not going there. It's water under the bridge."

Be willing to face it. Suffering, if left unprocessed, will turn to bitterness and become toxic. This will defile your life and all those whom your life impacts.

As a person God loves, He asks you to bring your suffering to Him. Pour out your heart and let Him lead you through a healing process. Find some caring people to support you, love you, and pray for you through all the pain and hurt. Let the Heavenly Father bring His supernatural peace to your heart and give you His eternal perspective, with the assurance that all of your why-questions will one day be answered.

A dear friend of ours is a living example of someone who has allowed God to redeem her suffering. She was fit, healthy, and led an active life. But four years ago, while walking, she accidentally and mysteriously fell.

Here's how she describes her first few weeks in the hospital:

My muscles went into painful contractions that didn't stop. My hand began to swell and turn a bluish colour. My whole right arm began to stiffen and no longer move. Confusing nerve messages messed with my brain and made me feel that my right arm and hand were in a different position and place. It was so odd. Each day the swelling and pain increased and made it impossible to move.

There was damage in my nervous system. My nerves were sending the wrong messages to the blood system. The constant cramping in my arms and legs was a sign that oxygen wasn't getting to my limbs as it should, and soon my legs were in constant pain, making it harder to walk. This all hit hard, as I love long-distance running. I love being active and living a healthy lifestyle. I loved being a massage therapist and helping people get well.

She was diagnosed as having a neurological condition called complex regional pain syndrome (CRPS) and is under the care of some good doctors who are specifically trained in this condition.

As you can imagine, many, many people have been praying for her and with her. While there has been some improvement over the years, she is still not completely healed... yet. We look forward to that day.

But read for yourself what she says about her journey of faith through these extremely difficult years of suffering:

Entering into suffering where pain never lets up day and night really forces you to either fully believe and embrace the truth about Jesus, or just give up. And during this pain-filled season of life, I truly have encountered the grace and love of God, which has made my heart become absolutely convinced and fully confident that God is *always* good, and *always* keeps His promises.

I experienced what it's like to cling to Jesus through sleepless nights and cry out His name in desperation. I felt Him hold me when no one else could because the pain was so intense.

I felt God's patience flow through me as I faced the daily reality of my cramped-down muscles. I encountered God's strength to not give up hope and keep dreaming despite the diagnoses of permanent damage.

I learned the importance of a grateful heart as God filled my heart with wonder for the many miraculous things He does each day. The most significant gift was understanding and truly experiencing the love of God in suffering.

The love of God in suffering. Remarkable! Only someone who has allowed God to redeem their suffering could write words like that. Her faith is growing as she allows the pain to drive her closer to the Father. She doesn't allow the pain to make her bitter or cause her to give up or stay isolated. Instead she processes her pain with strength from the Lord and support from His people and good doctors. God is using her story to inspire hope and faith in many people's lives.

Allowing God to redeem our suffering is often a long, challenging journey, but it is a journey the Lord invites us to take. He promises to walk with us every step of the way as He transforms what was meant to disable and cripple us into strengths He can use for His glory and for the sake of His Kingdom.

If you journey through your suffering with Him, God will give you a message and ministry to many others who are also suffering in this world.

Dear reader, why don't you consider praying about this right now?

Father, thank You for knowing what it's like to suffer, and for identifying with all my suffering. Thank You for Your compassion toward me. Thank You for taking all my past—with its wounds, hurts, sins, and failures—and redeeming it into something beautiful for Your Kingdom.

I give you my life, surrender my past, and ask You to take control of my future. Make me a living message of Your love and healing power.
In Jesus's name, amen.

Questions for Reflection

1. What pain and suffering in your life still needs to be processed redemptively with the help of the Lord and His people?
2. What steps do you need to take for that to happen?
3. What life message may God be developing in you through your greatest hurts and wounds?

WHO THE FATHER
SAYS YOU ARE
Chapter Twelve

Identity is everything. In fact, our perception of who we are determines how we live.

A few years ago, God gave me an insight into how identity works. As we all know, when you buy a new computer it comes with certain default settings from the factory. If you want, you can change this by personalizing those settings in a way that suits you.

In the same way, our lives are created with certain default settings put in place by God. These settings are positive and allow us to operate with the understanding that we are loved and have honour, value, and dignity.

Over time, however, these defaults can be altered by difficult experiences in life. Eventually we find ourselves operating out of a very different set of parameters than the ones we started with.

As a personal example, I've developed many alternate settings over the years that have strayed from God's default. These settings are based on the belief that I am weak and lack courage. They cause me to function out of the pressure to perform in order to gain approval and validation. They reveal my deep fear that I won't have enough money because I grew up in a poor family.

The Lord has shown me that He wants to access my settings menu, click on a tab called "God's Preferences," and reset who I am based on His truth about me. For example, He is helping me reset the "weak and fearful" setting to "strong and courageous" (Joshua 1:8). He is resetting the "performance" setting to "being accepted apart from what I do" (Romans 3:28) and training me in how to use this new mode. He is resetting "impoverished" and returning me to His original "provision" setting, with the assurance that He will provide for all my needs (Philippians 4:19).

God changes these settings through the process of renewing our minds (Romans 12:2). This is an ongoing process through which we must continually identify and reject the false settings we've adopted and replace them with the truth of God's default through prayer.

It takes time and intentionality to develop a new, biblical identity. This may seem like overwhelming and exhausting work—and it can be—but don't give up, even when your progress seems slow or stalled.

I encourage you to take the time to list those things that have become part of your alternate settings. These are the things that have been established through lies you've come to believe—lies about yourself that keep you bound in shame, fear, defeat, and unbelief. With this list before you, take time to ask the Lord to reveal His truth, which addresses those lies.

This is how we begin the process of restoring God's default settings in our hearts and minds.

Our Identity

Our identity determines how we relate to our Heavenly Father. Just as many people have a distorted view of the Father, formed by hurts and lies, others have a distorted view of themselves for similar reasons. Knowing our core identity as sons and daughters of the Father is imperative for us to be able to receive and experience His love.

Many people view themselves as unworthy of love because of negative filters in their lives. These are formed by their perceived shortcomings, failures, disappointments, and weaknesses, not to mention the hurtful things that have been said and done to them by others.

The Father wants us to discover the truth about who we are and how He sees us. There is tremendous freedom in believing who He says we are and living according to that truth. That's what this chapter is all about.

We're all on a lifelong search for our identity. Asking "Who am I?" isn't limited to young people trying to figure out their lives. It's a question we ask at every age. As we get older, the core question becomes "Who am I now?" Every new season of change and transition raises the question of our identity.

Whether we're older or younger, if we look to culture to answer this question we will develop a false identity based on constantly shifting values and circumstances. If we look to ourselves, we will develop an identity based on our limited self-perception (what we think we can do). If we look to others—parents, family members, teachers, friends, etc.—we will become enslaved to people's expectations, plans, and opinions of us.

While seeking an understanding of ourselves in all these areas is, to a degree, unavoidable, they all fall short of leading us to a true sense of identity. That is, unless Jesus Christ is at the centre of our search.

The search for identity is, in fact, a search for validation. Do I have what it takes? Am I adequate? Am I good enough? Am I loved for who I am? When we search for that validation from people, we never find a satisfying answer because all we receive is mixed messages. To some people, we're good enough; to others, we're not. We can never be quite sure.

The only source of true and lasting validation is the Heavenly Father. When we are anchored in the Father's voice of validation, the other voices in our lives become quieter and lose their power to falsely define us.

> LEARNING YOUR TRUE IDENTITY HAS EVERYTHING TO DO WITH WHO CHRIST IS, RATHER THAN WHO YOU ARE.

Would it surprise you if I said that knowing your true identity has very little to do with you? I can hear some of you saying, "But finding out who I am has *everything* to do with me!" Not so. What you will discover in this chapter is that learning your true identity has everything to do with who Christ is, rather than who you are.

Three Identity Keys

Let me share three key insights that will help us find our true identity in Christ. Don't rush through these sections. Read them through carefully.

I. God the Father. Our identity grows out of knowing God the Father's identity—His personality, nature and values. The first step in seeking out the answer to the question "Who am I?" is to pose a question to God the Father: "Who are You?"

This is what we encounter in John's gospel when Philip, on behalf of the disciples trying to figure out their identities in light of the revolutionary life and teaching of their Rabbi, made this request: *"Lord, show us the Father and that will be enough for us"* (John 14:8).

How could such an insight have satisfied the disciples' search—and ours today? Philip clued in to the fact that knowing who the Father is and what He has done provides a lens that ultimately brings our identity into focus. And as Jesus was faithful in revealing the Father and teaching His disciples about Him, so that same revelation is available to all who ask this question through the written word of the scriptures, particularly when those words are brought to life by the Spirit.

Unfortunately, most Christians miss this. They search the scriptures, eagerly seeking to find out what God says about who they are, but this never seems to produce a confident and secure self-identity. The mistake is to focus on ourselves when God wants us to first focus on who *He* is. This is the primary means through which the Father will shape our identity.

2. Jesus Christ. The second important insight is that our true identity can only be found in connection to Jesus Christ. While Jesus embodies the fullness of God's nature and personality (John 14:10–11), He also has established the means for us to live out of our God-given identity through His accomplished work on the cross.

Paul wrote, *"But now in Christ Jesus you who once were far away have been brought near by the blood of Christ"* (Ephesians 2:13). Outside of the redemptive work of Jesus Christ, we are unable to enter into the fullness of our God-given identity.

3. Holy Spirit revelation. The third important insight in discovering who we truly are is that our God-given identity is given to us by a revelation of the Holy Spirit, not through our own efforts or understanding.

Multitudes of Christians are familiar with the teachings of the Bible, yet not all experience genuine growth and transformation in their lives. Why is this? It's because the transformative truth about who we are in Christ requires a Spirit-given revelation. This is true of all scripture.

That's the point Paul made when he prayed for believers to be given *"the Spirit of wisdom and revelation. . . that the eyes of your heart may be enlightened in order that you may know the hope to which he has called you. . ."* (Ephesians 1:17–18)

Only the Holy Spirit can reveal truth to us by opening the eyes of our hearts. As a result, we not only come to know God better, we come to know *ourselves* better. Only the Spirit can show us who the Father is and reveal the work Christ has done for us so we can live out of our true identity. Jesus Himself said that *"the Spirit will receive from me what he will make known to you"* (John 16:15).

Only the Holy Spirit can reveal to us what it truly means to be in Christ.

What It Means to Be in Christ

"In Christ" is a key phrase that leads us to a discovery of our true identity. In the first two chapters of Ephesians, the phrases "in Christ," "in Him," "through Him," and "with Christ" are mentioned fourteen times. Paul repeatedly tells us who we are by using these phrases.

Implicit in this language is the fact that our identity is found in belonging to Christ, identifying with Him, and being in relationship with Him. Being in Christ is what gives us our true identity and changes our false settings back to God's true defaults.

Eight Identity Truths

With this in mind, let's look at several truths about our true identity from the first two chapters of Ephesians. Before looking at these truths, though, take time to pray that God's Spirit of wisdom and revelation will enlighten your heart to know Him and yourself better. Ask the Spirit to open the eyes of your heart and mind to understand what it means to be in Christ.

Truth 1: because you are in Christ, the Heavenly Father chose you. Ephesians 1:4 says, *"For he chose us in him before the creation of the world to be holy and blameless in his sight."*

You are chosen by the Father. This means that the Father knows you personally. He knows you by name. He has known you before the beginning of time. You were chosen by the Heavenly Father, who loved you before creation. You were known, planned for, and destined to be on this planet before creation took place. You're not here by accident, but by His design.

The lie·that many people choose to believe is that they are nobody, just a face in the crowd. They feel like they mean nothing to God, like He doesn't even know they exist. Because they don't matter to Him, it doesn't matter how they live or what they do; God won't notice anyway.

The truth is that God chose you by name to be on earth at this time in history to play a valuable part in His story. He chose you to be holy and set apart for Him, to be blameless and righteous in His sight.

This is your identity. This is who you are. You have been chosen by God. When the Spirit opens our eyes to this amazing truth, we are able to receive a deep sense of value and worth.

Truth 2: because you are in Christ, you are holy and blameless.

Ephesians 1:4 says, *"For he chose us in him before the creation of the world to be holy and blameless in his sight."*

You are holy and blameless in the Father's sight. That's right—holy and blameless! The Father sees you this way because that is how He sees Christ, and you are in Christ. What is true of Christ is now true of you.

The lie many choose to believe is that our current state of unholiness and sinfulness is who we are. We define ourselves by the sin and poor choices we make. We see many problems in our life for which we can be blamed. But that is not how the Father sees us.

The truth is that because of your faith in Jesus and the saving, cleansing work of His blood on the cross, you are now holy and blameless before the Father. You have received Christ's holy and righteous nature by faith. You have been "justified by His blood" (Romans 5:9), which means you are legally declared holy and righteous based on what Christ did for you on the cross.

What joy to realize that the Father doesn't reject us as sinful and fallen people, but fully accepts us as holy and blameless children.

Truth 3: because you are in Christ, the Heavenly Father adopted you. Ephesians 1:4–5 says, *"In love, he predestined us for adoption to sonship through Jesus Christ. . ."*

The Father has adopted you as His own child. You were handpicked by Him before time began to belong to Him as His child forever. God's decision to adopt you wasn't based on anything you have done or will do; it's entirely His choice to love you. The sad lie many people choose to believe is that they don't belong, that they're all alone in this life, an orphan without a home, abandoned with no one to look after them.

The Spirit wants to reveal to you that you are not an outsider, orphan, or misfit. You are welcomed, loved, and accepted as an adopted and celebrated member of God's family. You are a son or daughter of God. The Father has desired you from the beginning of time, and He still does.

Truth 4: because you are in Christ, the Heavenly Father has purchased you. Ephesians 1:7 says, *"In him we have redemption through his blood, the forgiveness of sins. . ."*

An item's value is determined by how much a person is willing to pay for it. Being in Christ means that you have been purchased, or redeemed, by the blood Jesus Christ poured out on the cross. You can't put a price on that! This means that all your sins—past, present, and future—have been forgiven. The Father doesn't hold your sins against you anymore because you are now in Christ. You are forgiven. All the sins and failures in your life, all the things you have done wrong, they are forgiven because of God's grace.

The lie many choose to believe is that they are unforgivable. What they have done is so bad that even God can't forgive them. Furthermore, many choose to believe the lie that they are losers, damaged goods, worthless and unwanted. They aren't worth being loved and feel like they don't matter to anyone. They believe that if people knew what they were really like, they would be rejected like yesterday's trash.

The Spirit wants to reveal to you the costly love and sacrifice that led to your total redemption and forgiveness. Just look at the price Jesus paid: His very own blood! In Christ, you have infinite worth. He gave Himself willingly by dying on the cross for you. The Father lovingly gave up His Son to die in your place and bear the punishment for your sin.

Over the years, I've shared this sweet story about a boy and his sailboat to illustrate the meaning of redemption.

A little boy worked long and hard to build a wooden sailboat. He loved that boat and was so proud of what he had made.

When it was finally ready, he took the boat to a nearby river and launched it into the water to see how it would sail. Suddenly, an unexpected breeze caught the sailboat and blew it far down the river. He ran hard, trying to catch it, but he couldn't reach it. The sailboat disappeared into the distance.

The boy was heartbroken. He had lost the boat he loved and had worked so hard to build.

Weeks later, as he walked past a second-hand shop in town, he saw his sailboat in the window. With great excitement, he ran into the shop and told the owner that it was his sailboat and reached up to take it home.

"That's my boat, son," said the shopkeeper. "I bought it from someone a few weeks ago. So if you want it, you'll have to pay for it."

Despite pleas from the boy, who even pointed out his initials carved on the bottom of the boat, the shopkeeper refused.

So the boy went home. He decided to earn enough money through work to buy back his boat—and finally the day arrived when he had saved the full purchase price. He walked into the store, paid the shopkeeper, and left with the biggest smile on his face, holding the boat he loved. This trophy was now his twice-owned boat—first because he had made it, and second because he had bought it.

Because we are in Christ, we are twice-owned, lovingly created by the Father and then redeemed by His Son, Jesus Christ. Because you are in Christ, you are God's very own priceless treasure.

Truth 5: because you are in Christ, the Heavenly Father has marked and sealed you. Ephesians 1:13–14 says, *"When you believed, you were marked in him with a seal, the promised Holy Spirit, who is a deposit guaranteeing our inheritance until the redemption of those who are God's possession—to the praise of his glory"* (Ephesians 1:13–14).

Being in Christ means that you were marked with the Holy Spirit as a seal of ownership, like the initials on the boat. The Holy Spirit's seal is an eternal promise that you belong to the Father and have a guaranteed heavenly inheritance waiting for you. You are God's possession, which brings Him great praise and glory.

The lie that many choose to believe is that they need to strive to stay in God's good books in order to be assured of a future heavenly inheritance. They believe that God is disapprovingly watching them, trying to decide whether or not He should keep them. They believe they need to prove their worthiness by their good life and deeds.

The Spirit wants to show you that the Father is pleased to mark you as His own child for all of eternity, based solely on His unconditional love.

All this is a result of being chosen, adopted, and purchased. This isn't about you and what you've done; it's about Jesus and what He's done. It's about being in Christ. He longs for you to feel eternally secure. The gift of the indwelling Holy Spirit is His way of saying, "You're Mine forever." The deposit of the Holy Spirit is a down-payment that anticipates the full inheritance we will receive in heaven.

Truth 6: because you are in Christ, the Heavenly Father has seated you with Christ in heavenly places. Ephesians 2:6 says, *"And God raised us up with Christ and seated us with him in the heavenly realms in Christ Jesus. . ."*

Even now, while you are still alive on the earth, the Father has seated you with Christ in heaven.

Being in Christ means that you can see things from a heavenly perspective. It's so easy to be overwhelmed by the things happening here in the world. If all we have is an earthly perspective, we'll easily lose hope and feel defeated. But when we recognize that we are seated with Christ in heaven, we are given a new heavenly perspective. We can see things from God's vantage point, which gives us hope, meaning, and faith.

Being in Christ also means that the Father has granted you the privilege of partnering with Jesus in ruling over the evil powers and principalities of this world.

This is about spiritual authority. He has given us authority along with Jesus to participate in the works of the Kingdom and defeat evil and darkness. The Spirit wants to reveal that Jesus is currently seated in authority above all the powers and principalities of darkness.

> . . .*[the Father] raised Christ from the dead and seated him at his right hand in the heavenly realms, far above all rule and authority, power and dominion, and every name that is invoked, not only in the present age but also in the one to*

come. And God placed all things under his feet and appointed him to be head over everything for the church.

—Ephesians 1:20–22

Jesus now rules from heaven and desires to share that position of authority with us today, not just when we get to heaven. Mind-blowing! No wonder we need the Spirit's revelation in order to begin to grasp the immensity of this truth.

The lie many Christians choose to believe is that they have no role to play in the spiritual world. They believe that the battle between good and evil, light and darkness, God and Satan takes place in a realm they have no business participating in. Except for a few prayers, they will stay on the sidelines and let God fight His own big battles.

Only through the revelation of the Spirit will we be able to see that being in Christ means we have been given spiritual authority. Because of Christ's victorious death and resurrection, the powers of sin, evil, and darkness have been defeated and we are able to share in that victory with Him in a Kingdom partnership.

This requires us to embrace the bold faith implicit in our God-given identity. Only with bold faith are we able to partner with Christ in His authority do the works of the Kingdom.

Truth 7: because you are in Christ, the Heavenly Father has planned good works for you. Ephesians 2:10 says, *"For we are God's handiwork, created in Christ Jesus to do good works, which God prepared in advance for us to do."*

Being in Christ means that the Father fashioned you for a special calling and assignment in your lifetime. You are His handiwork, meaning that you are a wonderfully created person, perfectly suited for what He has planned for you. He created you with the skills, personality, and gifts to accomplish the good works He prepared for you before creation.

There is no greater excitement than seeing the Father accomplish His plans through you. Your life won't be over until you have served God's purpose in your own generation (Acts 13:36). What an adventure!

Many people choose to believe the lie that they must find their own calling. Beware of a myth we hear more and more often these days—the myth of following your own dreams. This is the belief that you can become anything you set your mind to, that if you work hard enough you'll achieve your dreams. That's so misleading! This thinking is self-focused, not God-focused. We don't have the kind of power needed to fashion our own lives and become anything we want.

There's nothing wrong with hard work and having dreams, but all of this working and dreaming must be submitted to the Lordship of Jesus Christ. The truth is that God has a purpose and plan for your life and He is willing and eager to share it with you and equip you for the task. But it's *His* plan, not ours. We aren't meant to come up with a dream for our life apart from God's leading.

To discover His plan for us, we must first learn to submit our lives to His Lordship and follow Him every day in both the big and small details.

The Lordship of Christ means that Jesus is the King of our lives. Because He purchased and adopted us, He has every right to be in charge. He is a merciful, sovereign King, so we can joyfully surrender and submit to what He wants for us. His plans for us are always good.

Truth 8: because you are in Christ, the Heavenly Father gives you access to be close to Him. Ephesians 2:13, 18 says, *"But now in Christ Jesus you who once were far away have been brought near by the blood of Christ. . . For through him we both have access to the Father by one Spirit."*

Being in Christ means that we are given direct access to the presence of the Father through Christ, so we may draw close and approach Him with freedom, boldness, and confidence.

My immediate family has access to me. If they call me, I will respond no matter what I'm doing. I'm available to them because I love them and have given them priority access.

The Holy Spirit wants you to see how privileged you are in being given this kind of direct access to the Father. Believing God has given you this kind of access changes the way you pray, live, relate to people, and serve God. The Father welcomes you into His presence anytime for any reason. We can boldly draw near!

Many choose to believe the lie that they cannot come close to God and must remain distant. This is because of the negative filters discussed earlier in this chapter. Many people see themselves as sinful and unworthy, believing that God doesn't want anything to do with them. As a result, they resign themselves to a life of avoiding the Father and keeping Him at a distance.

Contrast this with the phrase *"brought near by the blood of Christ"* in Ephesians 2:13. His blood, shed on the cross, opened the way to the Father. You are welcomed by Him because Christ is welcomed, and you are in Christ. This is the reason you have access to the Father, *"by a new and living way opened for us through the curtain, that is, his body. . ."* (Hebrews 10:20)

You don't have to live at a distance from the Father anymore. The way to Him has been opened by Jesus.

Being in Christ means that you can be close to the Father, and stay close to Him. Think about it: the Father wants you near Him. He loves proximity, closeness, and intimacy. He welcomes you as a part of *"the people close to his heart"* (Psalm 148:14).

His arms are open, welcoming you and ready to hold you close in His loving embrace.

An Identity Hit

During the writing of this chapter, my identity took a hit by the old, familiar feeling of rejection.

As I approached my sixty-fifth birthday, I was struck by the fear that not many people would attend the party my wife had planned, that it would be smaller than I had hoped. You have to understand that I'm an off-the-charts people person. Being with lots of people energizes me—the more people, the happier I am.[15]

A deep depression began to settle over me. Again, I started to believe the lie that people don't like me enough to make the effort to come. At the time, we were still living under COVID restrictions and people were quite cautious about gathering in groups, even outdoors. Though I understood this, I still felt sorry for myself.

So I talked to the Lord about it. Here's what He said to me.

---

15 Side note: Audrey is the polar opposite. She's a one-on-one, or one-on-two person. Being around lots of people exhausts her.

"Bobby, I know it hurts when you want lots of people to be at your party and it doesn't happen. But you're being too self-focused. People do love you and celebrate you. But more importantly, *I* love you and celebrate you. My feelings toward you should matter more than any other person's feelings. I'm the Person who loves you most and I'm going to be at your party. Here's what you need to know: the way I love My Son, Jesus, is the way I love you, My son, Bobby. When I said to Jesus, 'With you I am well pleased,' I was saying it to you. I could have said I was merely pleased with you, but instead I said, 'I am well pleased with you.' That's more than pleased. Super pleased. Now believe this and accept it from My heart to yours."

Wow! I was touched deeply. My Father is so good to me!

I'm happy to report that the spirit of rejection began to lift shortly after this conversation with the Father, and I looked forward to a smaller but still wonderful and joy-filled sixty-fifth birthday party.

As it turned out, the party went great. I am so thankful for the people who did come, including my entire family, which means everything to me.

A Time to Respond

Your identity has been established by God, in Christ, and revealed by the Holy Spirit. Being in Christ is the key. You are chosen, holy and blameless, adopted, purchased, forgiven, marked and sealed, seated in heavenly places, created for good works, close to the Father.

Which of the identity truths in this chapter impact you the most? Why? What has the Holy Spirit highlighted to you that He wants to further develop in your identity as a dearly loved child of the Father?

Dear reader, may your identity in Christ be fully formed so that you can stay anchored to your true identity throughout your life.

Father, thank You for who You are and for who I am. Thank You for making me the way You did and forming my identity in Christ. Help me to know who I am, like who I am, and be who I am. Knowing that You, Father, are well pleased with me makes all the difference. I want to embrace my identity in Christ with joy and gratitude. I love You, Father.

In Jesus's name, amen.

Questions for Reflection

1. Take the time to list those things that have become part of your alternate default settings, established through the lies you have come to believe about yourself. With this list before you, ask the Lord to reveal His truth which addresses each of those lies. In prayer, renounce those lies and declare God's truth in their place. This will take a considerable investment of thought, prayer, and time.
2. How is being "in Christ" the key to discovering our true identity?
3. Of the several identity truths mentioned, which ones impact you the most? Why? Which ones does the Holy Spirit want to further develop in you? Who are the people who can journey with you through this process?

HEALING FOR FATHER WOUNDS

Chapter Thirteen

Most people have experienced some degree of wounding from their father or mother, or from a significant adult in their life. However, for the purposes of this chapter, I will be using the term "father wounds" to encompass all of these.

As you read earlier, I experienced profound wounding by my earthly father. I am so grateful for the healing I have received from the Lord. He has entered into the places of pain, shame, and lies and restored my soul in many ways.

The Heavenly Father offers you healing from your father wounds. Without His healing, we will continually struggle to receive and experience God's love.

Here is a story from a friend who experienced progressive healing from her father wound over a number of years:

My parents had their own wounds and traumas that had not really been talked about or processed when I was born. This led to a tumultuous marriage and I often got emotionally drawn in to the pain and chaos that existed between them.

My dad was a kind man, but quite distant emotionally. This meant I didn't feel affirmed or confident of where I stood with guys and men. In my early twenties, I began to seek out help and healing. That help included a wonderful long-term counsellor, some group therapy, books and teachings, finding safe and healthy friends who were also on their own journey towards wholeness, and good community—both inside and outside of the church.

In my thirties, I went overseas to work. I strongly felt God tell me (and confirmed through an older friend) that He was going to move heaven and earth to change my relationships with men.

During many quiet nights while I was away, I had these encounters where I could see Jesus looking into my eyes. He was imparting to me a deep sense of "I see you" and "I know you"—just like a dad does with his baby. I could also see in those eyes of liquid love a Man who deeply identified with all my hurt and suffering. This was profound, beautiful, and life-changing—exactly what my heart and soul had been looking for.

When I returned, my dad came to visit me. I remember the old feelings of unresolved longing creeping back in, until the Holy Spirit reminded me that what I was looking for was now mine in my Heavenly Dad.

I felt a deep sense of freedom that night as I visited with my dad. Interestingly, it also changed how I felt about being single and brought a much deeper acceptance of who I was—with or without a husband. For the next six months, I was often moved to tears of gratitude at this new Daddy revelation that God had brought into my life. It was more than Father, it was Daddy, because the little girl in me had encountered a truly safe and present Dad who was excited to be with her.

My sister even commented that I seemed "more lighthearted" around my dad. This couldn't have been more true—because God had not only lifted a burden of longing from me, but He had filled me with His presence in a much more substantial, tangible way.

In this chapter, we will discuss several important steps you can take in order to find true and lasting healing from your father wounds.

Admit You Have a Father Wound

Our journey of healing begins with admitting that we do, indeed, carry a father wound. This may sound obvious, but it's not easy for everyone. Some people believe that if they think or say negative things about their fathers, they're disrespecting them and not honouring them as the Bible commands.

But that is not the case at all. The first step in the healing of father wounds is to acknowledge the hurt your father caused you, not for the purpose of blame but in order to identify the specific area of healing that you need.

Some people offer excuses for their father's sins and failures. But each time we excuse sin, whether in ourselves or others, we avoid the opportunity to deal with that sin, and freedom eludes us. Every time we choose to bury sin, overlook it, or whitewash it, we remain in agreement with that sin and reinforce its power over us.

I've heard people say, "The past is the past. What's done is done. What's the point of bringing it up now? I'm over it." This is usually a clear indication that they are not over it—the past is still affecting their lives. We can only be healed from a father wound to the degree that we are willing to take it seriously and deal with it specifically.

Every time we expose sin, specifically identify it, and bring it into the light and to the cross of Jesus Christ we are able to receive healing. It is the shed blood of Jesus that brings wholeness and forgiveness and breaks the stronghold of the sin committed against us.

Some people believe they deserve the pain their father caused them, that it's their fault they were hurt by their father. They believe they should have been a better child and not have aggravated their father the way they did. They feel they don't deserve to be forgiven or healed.

Let me say as strongly as possible: *you are not responsible for the way your father, or anyone else, hurt you.* Stop blaming yourself. Acknowledge the sin committed against you and choose to forgive the person who hurt you. This is how to receive the healing God wants to bring you.

> YOU ARE NOT RESPONSIBLE FOR THE WAY YOUR FATHER, OR ANYONE ELSE, HURT YOU.

Jesus asked the lame man at the pool of Bethesda, *"Do you want to get well?"* (John 5:6) You may think this question would be a no-brainer for someone living with a lifelong physical ailment.

Jesus puts this same question to us who live with chronic emotional, mental, and spiritual ailments stemming from the wounds of our past. Many people aren't willing to fully deal with their hurt and pain. Some flatly deny there's any problem at all. Others give the impression that they're willing to deal with their wounds, but they want to do it on their own terms and be in control of the process. In so doing, they derail that process.

So, do you want to get well? That is the all-important question. You have to be willing to fully surrender to Jesus's healing process and accept His terms. It's so important to face this question honestly by asking the Lord to show you any areas of unwillingness, hesitancy, or hiding in your life—and the reason for it.

Many people will not be ready to deal with their wounds *until the pain of remaining wounded becomes greater than the pain of being healed*. And there is pain in being healed. This means facing some very hurtful memories. Many people want a Band-aid solution instead of spiritual surgery. A quick fix is a guarantee that you'll stay broken.

Some who have been wounded for many years prefer to remain a victim and hold on to the hurt done to them as an excuse for not getting better. They've learned to live with their brokenness as a normal way of life and are afraid of learning to live as a healed person.

Many people feel sorry for a victim, so living wounded can become a convenient place to hide and an excuse for staying broken. Part of growing up and maturing in Christ is taking responsibility for your healing and spiritual growth.

God's desire for His children is for us to live healed and whole. He doesn't see us as victims, but as *"more than conquerors"* (Romans 8:37). He certainly feels compassion for your wounds and brokenness, but He doesn't want you to remain there. He sees you for what He made you to be and the destiny He has prepared for you.

When the angel of God met Gideon fearfully threshing wheat in a winepress, the angel didn't focus on his fear and reluctance. He affirmed Gideon for the person he would become. The angel told him, *"The Lord is with you, mighty warrior"* (Judges 6:12). Imagine that! "Mighty warrior." This was the prophetic word of the Lord to a cowering, fearful person.

Are you willing to admit that you need healing? Are you able to tell God that you want to get better and commit yourself to a journey of deep, inner healing? Please take some time right now to ask Jesus to help you face your wounds and begin the journey of healing with Him.

Twenty Minutes to Nine

In Charles Dickens's novel *Great Expectations*, we are introduced to a character named Miss Havisham. She is a rich old lady living alone in a luxurious house, a mansion that has become her prison. The windows are boarded up, so the house is always dark. All the clocks are frozen in time, having been purposely set at exactly twenty minutes to nine.

Miss Havisham still wears the dress from a wedding day that never happened. Instead of glistening white, the dress has wrinkled, faded, and become yellow. The woman wearing the dress has likewise withered and shrunken to skin and bones. She wears only one shoe on her feet.

I won't give away exactly what happens, but she clearly suffered a great trauma on the morning of her wedding. It was so traumatic that her life literally froze—at twenty minutes to nine. She has been stuck in that painful place for many years, refusing to move beyond the wound she received.

Many Christians are stuck in their spiritual growth because they aren't able to deal with a traumatic event in their past. They're unable or unwilling to face the pain of that event, so they have lost the desire to deal with it. As a result, they find it hard to connect with God's love, as well as the love of other people.

The good news is that you don't have to stay stuck in your trauma. You can find much grace from God and gentle help from His people to move beyond whatever pain has you frozen in the past.

What would it take for you to be willing to deal with your past wounds? One of the greatest incentives is desiring not to pass on the effects of those wounds to the next generation. The unhealthy patterns in our lives need to be faced and healed so our children and grandchildren can be free of them. This is what God wants.

Questions to Begin the Process

Here are a few questions about your father or mother that you need to answer honestly. Carefully think through these questions. It may be helpful to write out your answers.

What kind of father did you have growing up? Similar to what I asked in Chapter One, was he distant, passive, withdrawn, demanding, authoritarian, angry, abusive, or absent, either emotionally or physically? Or was he loving, kind, and encouraging? An even-tempered disciplinarian? Was he fun, godly, and emotionally attentive and available to you? Did he ever say "I love you"?

Perhaps you had no father at all, like me. In all likelihood, your father was probably a combination of many things, both good and bad.

In what ways were you hurt by your father? It's important to answer this question without minimizing the hurt.

In what ways are you like/unlike your father? This helps expose the sinful and broken patterns that God wants to heal so you and future generations can live in freedom.

How has the relationship with your father affected the relationship with your Heavenly Father? It's important to see this connection so that you can repent of, renounce, and replace the broken and sinful patterns that you have transferred from your father to the Heavenly Father.

For example, those who grow up with a demanding, performance-oriented father may think they need to work harder and be a better person in order to please their Heavenly Father and earn His approval. Those with an absent or distant father may think that God isn't interested in them or doesn't care for them, so they develop a life of self-reliance and independence.

If you have closed your heart to your father in order to protect yourself from further pain, it's possible you have also closed your heart to the Heavenly Father. You need to ask God if this is true.

We may have put up shields to protect us from further hurt, but as Rob Reimer wisely writes, "The problem with shields is they are indiscriminate—they not only block out the person who is hurting us, they also block out God from healing us."[16]

---

16 Reimer, *Soul Care*, 192.

Admitting the need for healing is crucial. This is the starting point for getting healed of our father wounds. Prayer for healing needs to be specific and thorough. Full disclosure leads to full healing.

Sexual abuse by a father, or any other person, creates some of the deepest wounds a person can experience. If you have been victimized in this way, your Heavenly Father's heart feels your pain and is moved with compassion for you. He desires to give you an encounter with His love so you can be healed, cleansed, and set free to discover safety and intimacy with Him and others.

This kind of healing will take time, as God gently wants to heal the layers of woundedness you may be carrying. You will certainly need the loving care of an experienced, godly counsellor and trusted intercessors in your journey of healing.

God is also a God of justice. If the abuse has crossed any legal boundaries and the abuser has not been held to account with the law, the authorities need to be notified. This is a legitimate and important step that can be crucial to one's journey of healing.

Believe that Jesus Wants and Is Able to Heal You

A man with leprosy came and knelt before him and said, "Lord, if you are willing, you can make me clean."

Jesus reached out his hand and touched the man. "I am willing," he said. "Be clean!" Immediately he was cleansed of his leprosy.

—Matthew 8:2–3

I love this story of a man with leprosy who came to Jesus to be healed. Many can relate to asking Jesus for healing only to wonder if anything will happen. They wonder, *Will God actually heal me? Is Jesus willing, or will I just go away disappointed?*

This same doubt keeps many of us from praying for other people's healing.

Instead of letting these fears and doubts control us, Jesus invites us to come to Him with a childlike heart of faith and ask for healing. What God does in response to these prayers is determined by His sovereign, loving plans and purposes for our lives.

We often make healing prayer too much about ourselves. We fear embarrassment or disappointment that our prayer may not be answered. But the truth is that healing prayer isn't about us; it's about God, our Sovereign Healer.

In all the years I have prayed for people to be healed, whether they're healed in the way we hoped or not, something good always happens to them. They have felt loved and cared for by those who prayed for them. They have had an experience of the love and compassion of God through the prayers of His people. Sometimes healing comes immediately—and this is cause for much rejoicing. At other times, healing comes later or in a different way than what was asked. This is also a reason to rejoice! All of this is an act of faith to believe that God is good, and that He hears and acts on our prayers out of His mercy and compassion.

Seek Prayer Ministry from Others

While it's good to pray on our own for healing, we can miss out on a great source of God's healing power if we don't let others pray for us. Jesus makes the case for the value and effectiveness of being prayed for by others:

> *Again, truly I tell you that if two of you on earth agree about anything they ask for, it will be done for them by my Father in heaven. For where two or three gather in my name, there am I with them.*
> —Matthew 18:19–20

One of my favourite passages on healing can be found in the book of James. It further emphasizes the importance of praying with others:

> *Is anyone among you sick? Let them call the elders of the church to pray over them and anoint them with oil in the name of the Lord. And the prayer offered in faith will make the sick person well; the Lord will raise them up. If they have sinned, they will be forgiven. Therefore confess your sins to each other and pray for each other so that you may be healed. The prayer of a righteous person is powerful and effective.*
> —James 5:14–16

We must resist the inner lies that lead us to avoid asking others to pray for us. We may believe that our need isn't important enough, that people don't have the time, or that they don't really care. We say to ourselves, "I don't want to be vulnerable. Nothing will happen anyway."

Instead of listening to those lies, by faith and in obedience to Jesus's words, ask a few godly people you trust to pray for you in person. I've seen so many great things happen when God's people obey His direction and prompting in prayer.

Invite Jesus into the Wound/Painful Memory

When it comes to the healing of father wounds, an effective prayer strategy is to revisit the painful memory and engage the Father in a conversation about it.[17]

I can tell you with certainty that Jesus was there with you in that painful place and He wants to show you His loving presence. Psalm 139 teaches that God is with us everywhere, even in the dark places of hurt, sin, and pain:

> *Where can I go from your Spirit? Where can I flee from your presence? If I go up to the heavens, you are there; if I make my bed in the depths, you are there. If I rise on the wings of the dawn, if I settle on the far side of the sea, even there your hand will guide me, your right hand will hold me fast. If I say, "Surely the darkness will hide me and the light become night around me," even the darkness will not be dark to you; the night will shine like the day, for darkness is as light to you.*
> —Psalm 139:7–12

As you recall the occasion of your wounding, ask some specific questions of Jesus. Here are some helpful questions to ask Him in this place of painful memories:

- Where were You when I was being hurt?
- How were You feeling when I was experiencing this?

---

17 For some, the concept of engaging with God through modes of conversation and revisiting memories may seem unfamiliar. I recommend reading helpful books to build an understanding of listening prayer ministry. See the bibliography section at the end of the book for suggested resources.

• What do You want to say to me about what happened?

This form of seeking God's healing can be difficult and must be handled with gentleness and care. It should not be forced or manipulated. Also bear in mind that this may be a process that requires extended dialogue, prayer, and other support.

We should always pray for God's spiritual protection before engaging in this kind of prayer. When Jesus leads someone into a painful memory, His presence is able to help them feel safe.

Forgive, Forgive, and Forgive Again

Forgiveness is the key to healing. There can be no lasting healing without it. In declaring forgiveness for the offender, you aren't condoning their hurtful actions. You aren't letting them off the hook and allowing them to get away with their offence.

Rather, you're releasing yourself from being their judge and jury, and placing them into God's hands to deal with them as a just and righteous Judge.

Author Lewis B. Smedes, who has written extensively on the subject of forgiveness, offers this powerful insight: "When we forgive, we set a prisoner free and then discover that the prisoner we set free was us."[18]

Forgiveness is a process. Depending on the degree of hurt inflicted on someone, it may take a great deal of time before a person who has forgiven their offender can experience freedom from the pain evoked by the hurtful memory. Forgiveness may need to be declared many times.

> *Then Peter came to Jesus and asked, "Lord, how many times shall I forgive my brother or sister who sins against me? Up to seven times?"*
>
> *Jesus answered, "I tell you, not seven times, but seventy-seven times."*
>
> —Matthew 18:21–22

---

18 Lewis B. Smedes, *Forgive and Forget: Healing the Wounds We Don't Deserve* (New York, NY: Harper Collins, 1984), 24.

Choosing to *not* forgive the person who wounded you can lead to the development of a bitter root of judgment which is toxic to your soul, even affecting those around you (Hebrews 12:15).

Unforgiveness restricts the flow of God's mercy into your life, as told in Jesus's parable of the unmerciful servant (Matthew 18:23–35). Forgiveness, on the other hand, restores the flow of God's mercy into your life along with His life-giving presence.

You'll know you're walking in forgiveness when you can think of the person who hurt you without stirring up a flood of anger, bitterness, or hurt in your heart. You'll know you're free when you can pray for that person and bless them.

This doesn't mean that we abandon healthy boundaries placed around those still in our lives who have inflicted wounds upon us. Instead it means that we release them to God's mercy and justice rather judging and condemning them ourselves. Jesus said, *"But to you who are listening I say: Love your enemies, do good to those who hate you, bless those who curse you, pray for those who mistreat you"* (Luke 6:27–28).

Steps To Forgiveness

Here's an important question: how do you forgive a person who has wounded you? You can take some practical steps when you're ready and willing to enter the process of forgiveness. The place to begin is by acknowledging the hurt that was done to you. Don't minimize, excuse, or deny it. Meet with someone you trust and tell them what happened and how you feel. More importantly, tell Jesus how you feel and ask Him to help you work through the forgiveness process. He is more than ready, willing, and able to answer your prayer.

Then revisit the cross of Jesus Christ and remember His great love and forgiveness for you. Thank Jesus for the forgiveness and mercy (*hesed*) He has freely given you. Read the story of His crucifixion and hear Him say the words, *"Father, forgive them, for they do not know what they are doing"* (Luke 23:34). Ask Jesus how He feels about the person who hurt you and how He sees that person.

Now, in prayer, declare forgiveness for the person. It is helpful to pray aloud with one or two others. A wise, trusted friend can help encourage and coach you through this process, not to mention pray for you throughout.

Make sure you specifically state the name of the person you're forgiving and for what offence. "Father, I forgive _____ for _____." This is a very important step! Repeat this prayer for each person who has hurt you and for each offence. If it's too overwhelming, you don't have to cover every offence in one prayer session.

I cannot overemphasize the importance of specific prayer when it comes to declaring forgiveness. Vague, general prayers can be ineffective and indicate a reluctance to engage with the process. A specific prayer spoken in Jesus's name in agreement with one or more trusted friends has Christ's promise of effectiveness and spiritual authority. Matthew 18:19 says, *"Again, truly I tell you that if two of you on earth agree about anything they ask for, it will be done for them by my Father in heaven."*

Don't rush through this process. Remember that it takes time to forgive, depending on the severity of the hurt done to you. These steps are not a quick and easy process. It may be necessary to repeat this as often as you need, with others who care for you.

A Forgiveness Story

I'll never forget the visible change I saw in a woman from my former church who was able to forgive her father after she experienced the love of the Heavenly Father. She had grown up with a horribly abusive father and suffered deep, long-term wounds as a result. She hated him with a passion and believed she could never forgive him—nor should she! You could see this hatred in her countenance. Her face reflected years of bitterness, anger, and hurt.

Shortly after she started attending our church, she personally encountered the love of Christ, experienced His forgiveness for her sins, and became a Christian. It was a new beginning in her life, but she still had a difficult journey ahead.

At a weekend retreat, the Lord revealed to her that she needed to forgive her father. Understandably, she greatly struggled with this idea. God was inviting her to cross a bridge to be able to experience joy and peace she had never known before. But she had set up camp on her side of the bridge and was comfortable in her experience of a wounded, unforgiving life.

As part of the retreat, we took time to pray over her for the filling of the Holy Spirit. As we prayed, she was touched deeply by the love of God. She described it as

a refreshing chill that went right through me. I felt lifted off the floor. I wanted to dance and sing. I experienced such joy and freedom and kept saying, "I'm a new person. I have a Father, a Heavenly Father who loves me! He's my Father!"

As a result of this encounter, she was able to cross the bridge in her heart that she had resisted for so long. And for the first time she forgave her father.

One of the amazing results was the immediate change in her appearance. Her whole countenance was transformed. Her face, which had worn a perpetual scowl, was changed into one of radiant joy. We didn't know how beautiful her smile was until that day!

Shortly after this, this woman was baptized, and she continues to smile and walk in freedom and joy. There is great healing and freedom in forgiveness.

Participate in Christian Community and Minister to Others

There is no better way to walk in long-term healing than with a group of loving brothers and sisters in Christ who will support you through the healing process and beyond.

We make the mistake of going through this alone when God has provided caring people through whom we can gain support, perspective, and strength. Part of our healing journey in community is about helping others with their own healing. God heals us so we can also help others find their healing.

Praise be to the God and Father of our Lord Jesus Christ, the Father of compassion and the God of all comfort, who comforts us in all our troubles, so that we can comfort those in any trouble with the comfort we ourselves receive from God.
—2 Corinthians 1:3–4

Fixating on ourselves and our problems is sure to keep us stunted in our spiritual growth. God asks us to focus on others and be willing to help and serve where we can. This is essential for spiritual growth and strength. Ask God to show you whom you can love, serve, and pray for, and then let Him use you.

Dear reader, healing can be painful, but the results are worth it. We need to be intentional and determined to walk through the healing process, and not give up when it gets difficult or seems to take too long. Focus on your Heavenly Father and persevere. As you do, allow God to surround you with caring people who will hold you up as God lifts you out of your pain. He will show you who you are in Christ and help you to walk in freedom and joy.

I'd like to pray for you:

Father, please heal those who are carrying wounds from their father, or from someone else. Help them to courageously begin the healing journey with You, or to continue it.

I bring before you their hurts, pains, wounds—all the evil done to them. I ask in the strong name of Jesus Christ that Your healing power now be poured out upon them.

Father, You love them with an everlasting love. You are a compassionate Father who carries us all in Your arms. Jesus, You are the Good Shepherd who heals Your wounded sheep and finds those who are lost. Heal Your beloved people. In Jesus's name, amen.

Questions for Reflection

1. Please answer the following questions about your father/mother honestly. In what ways were you hurt by your father/mother? In what ways are you like or unlike your father/mother? How has the relationship with your father/mother affected the relationship with your Heavenly Father?

2. Where are you at in the process of healing from your father/mother wounds?

3. Which of the steps to healing do you need to take? Whose help do you need?

A CALL FOR SPIRITUAL
MOTHERS AND FATHERS
Chapter Fourteen

G rowing older is such a blessing! God honours those who are getting on in years. As Proverbs 20:29 tells us, "The glory of young men is their strength, gray hair the splendor of the old." God also promises fruitfulness and vitality in old age. We read in Psalm 92, "The righteous will flourish like a palm tree, they will grow like a cedar of Lebanon... They will still bear fruit in old age, they will stay fresh and green..." (Psalm 92:12, 14) As we get older and mature, we have the opportunity to become a blessing to those who are younger.

Sadly, old age isn't always honoured or valued in our culture. Elderly people are often viewed as having little worth, an annoyance whose best days are behind them, a burden to tolerate until they die. Along with that, older people themselves can become selfish, critical, grumpy, and give up serving God and others.

God has a different vision for His older children.

There is a significant need

> AS WE GET OLDER AND
> MATURE, WE HAVE
> THE OPPORTUNITY TO
> BECOME A BLESSING
> TO THOSE WHO ARE
> YOUNGER.

for mature women and men to become spiritual mothers and fathers, or spiritual older sisters and brothers. The younger generation longs for older women and men who will love them, mentor them, pray for them, and be a steady influence in their lives as they navigate an unknown future. They long for spiritual parents. Spiritual parents don't have to be in their senior years. This calling can be lived out by people of all ages; there is always someone needing love and nurture.

*Even if you had ten thousand guardians in Christ, you do not have many fathers,
for in Christ Jesus I became your father through the gospel. Therefore I urge you
to imitate me.*

—I Corinthians 4:15–16

God uses seasoned women and men to pour out His heart of love to
the next generation. The Father heart of God is demonstrated and imparted
through women and men who themselves have experienced His heart of love.

One of the great lessons of maturity in the Christian life is to realize
that whatever God does in you, it's not just for you. He gives you gifts,
insights, and blessings so that you can pass them on to others. As Jesus
reminds us, *"Freely you have received; freely give"* (Matthew 10:8).

This role of nurture, care, and support for younger people is a ministry
that finds you. You don't have to look very far. The need is so great.

If you're open to this call, God will bring people into your life, showing
both of you that He has divinely orchestrated this relationship. You can call
it mentoring, spiritual friendship, or whatever you want. It can be formal or
casual—either way, it is a spiritual relationship through which God imparts
blessing to both parties.

There are many parental wounds in younger generations, and many of
these wounds can be healed by the Lord with the help of godly women and
men who will take the time to show God's unconditional love.

Learning how to speak a blessing to someone is a great gift from God.
Speaking a blessing, in its simplest form, means telling a person what you
appreciate about them, the qualities you see in them, and how God wants to
use them for His purposes. This doesn't have to be formal or rehearsed. As
a matter of fact, an encouraging word from the Holy Spirit spontaneously
given to a person can be powerful and life-changing.

The Simplicity of Spiritual Parenthood

Now that I'm in my mid-sixties and actively retired, one of the greatest blessings of my life is the younger people God has called me to love, befriend, and
mentor. They give me such joy with their questions, openness, gifts, humour,
insight, and zeal. What a great privilege it is to help them through their

sorrows and struggles, as well as to celebrate their joys and victories. What an honour to see them grow and become strong in the Lord and then find other younger people to reproduce the process!

In my experience, this process is surprisingly simple.

A young man approached me one Sunday morning after I had used a number of different guitars as an object lesson in a sermon. He came up and asked if I would teach him to play the guitar.

"Are you willing to work hard and practice?" I asked.

He said that he was.

This began a weekly rhythm of getting together for guitar lessons. The young man made good on his promise and quickly developed into a capable musician.

At the end of each lesson, I suggested we take a few minutes to pray together. This led to increased openness between us as we shared struggles, joys, and other things that were happening in our lives. It became a regular practice of learning from and ministering to each other. Over time, we both recognized the spiritual father/son connection which had formed. We cherish it to this day.

All of this was fostered through these simple times spent together each week.

Recently, after one of our lessons, I sent him a text: "I can't thank you enough for last night's conversation. It was SO encouraging! This morning I re-read the verse that you gave me, and it is God's clear word to me. Thank you for letting God speak through you!"

He responded by thanking me for giving him "a father's blessing."

These were simple words on my part, but they made a significant impact on him. Such a simple, loving, genuine father's blessing and word of encouragement can have a great influence in a person's life over time. It's simply a matter of loving someone and finding ways to express that love with affirming, Spirit-given words.

Biblical Profile of a Spiritual Mother/Father

What does it look like to be a spiritual mother or father? A survey of the Bible gives us seven primary characteristics that describe a spiritual parent.

I. Comfort and care. Isaiah 66:13 says, *"As a mother comforts her child, so will I comfort you..."* And we read in I Thessalonians 2:7–8, *"Just as a nursing mother cares for her children, so we cared for you."*

Childhood, whether physically or spiritually, is fraught with unknowns and struggles. There is no more basic a need for any child than comfort and care along this challenging journey.

A loving person naturally offers comfort. Spiritual parents have the opportunity to feel the Father's heart of love for their sons and daughters and to express it directly, openly, and generously. Likewise, care is the practical outworking of this same impulse—the desire to tangibly support those we are journeying with in whatever way they need.

2. Compassion. Isaiah 49:15 says, *"Can a mother forget the baby at her breast and have no compassion on the child she has borne?"*

Along the bumpy road of childhood, children have a natural inclination to fear that they will be forgotten and unseen. Compassion is the natural response of a healthy parent toward the child they love—an impulse that communicates "I see you. You matter!" This is the impulse reflected in the rhetorical question posed in Isaiah 49.

For younger people to develop compassionate love, they must experience compassionate love—the genuine, heartfelt love of a spiritual parent taking interest in their uniqueness and individual beauty, communicating value to them.

3. Close connection. We read in I Thessalonians 2:8, *"Because we loved you so much, we were delighted to share with you not only the gospel of God but our lives as well."*

Spiritual mothers and fathers are willing to get close to their sons and daughters who are looking for authentic relationships in which life can be openly and mutually shared. Keeping a safe distance from your son or daughter limits a parent's ability to have a positive impact on their lives.

Spiritual parents cannot settle for anything less than a close connection. This standard of connection comes from the heart of Jesus who *"became flesh and made his dwelling among us"* (John 1:14). The Father loves a close connection with His children.

Some people are afraid of this kind of closeness because their weaknesses and inadequacies may be exposed. But this kind of honesty is a great gift to your spiritual son or daughter! If we always project strength and confidence, and share only success stories, we rob them of learning how to deal with doubts, sins, and failures.

Another reason that some parents avoid close connection is that they fear developing an unhealthy dependency in their spiritual child. But this is unlikely to happen if a spiritual parent fosters a healthy dependency on God through their relationship, directing their son or daughter to seek everything they need from Him.

4. Co-labouring. Philippians 2:22 says, *"But you know that Timothy has proved himself, because as a son with his father he has served with me in the work of the gospel."*

Spiritual parents pass on wisdom and experience to their sons and daughters through partnering together in the work of the Kingdom. There's nothing like working and serving alongside each other!

In this context, spiritual parents and their children can learn from one another. The willingness to be a learner as well as a teacher is an important posture for spiritual parents to take. It's not a one-way relationship. There is so much to learn from the next generation.

5. Challenging. We read in 1 Thessalonians 2:11–12, *"For you know that we dealt with each of you as a father deals with his own children, encouraging, comforting and urging you to live lives worthy of God, who calls you into his kingdom and glory."*

Urging spiritual sons and daughters to live lives worthy of the gospel is a key element of being a spiritual parent—to call them onward and upward in their faith. In contrast to some people's assumptions, I have found that many younger people *want* to be challenged and stretched. They long for seasoned people to help them find a compelling vision of all they could become in Christ.

Spiritual parents shouldn't be afraid to challenge their spiritual sons and daughters to grow. They should be willing to work with them to develop a plan, and be patient with them as they learn how to implement it. This is accomplished not only by instruction but also by demonstration of their own willingness to stretch and grow.

Many older people feel they have nothing to offer, which often discourages them from taking up the call to be spiritual parents. But the Lord is inviting each of us to bring our small lunch of five loaves and two fishes to Him and let Him multiply its impact!

6. Cheering. Let's revisit this phrase from 1 Thessalonians 2:12: *"encouraging, comforting and urging you to live lives worthy of God..."*

Most parents know what it's like to cheer for their child at a sporting event. A parent naturally desires to shout encouragement and urge their child to do well on the playing field.

In a similar way, the next generation of Jesus-followers needs to be cheered on by those who've already been on the playing field of God's Kingdom. There is nothing more empowering to a younger disciple than having an older disciple who enthusiastically urges them to grow and succeed and be victorious in the journey of following Christ.

Audrey and I are passionate about seeing the next generation of leaders surpass us in gifts, skills, anointing, and power in the work of the Kingdom. To that end, our role as spiritual parents is not only to be good role models and to challenge the younger generation, but also to cheer them on.

Years ago, Audrey received a vision of us as an older generation of leaders humbly kneeling down before the Lord so that the next generation can climb on our shoulders and move further and higher in faith than we ever did. Lord, may that be so!

7. Confronting and correcting. Hebrews 12:5–6 says, *"And have you completely forgotten this word of encouragement that addresses you as a father addresses his son? It says, 'My son, do not make light of the Lord's discipline, and do not lose heart when he rebukes you, because the Lord disciplines the one he loves, and he chastens everyone he accepts as his son.'"*

I am so encouraged to see how many younger people want to be called out and have their sins, shortcomings, and blind spots pointed out. They want someone in their life to be honest and lovingly say the hard things. This sacred entrustment is available to spiritual parents. Words of correction, however, will only be received if people know that they are loved and their spiritual parent has their good at heart.

People commonly fear that corrective words will offend another—that it will drive the person away. The truth is that younger people deeply respect those older ones who will speak the hard word of truth in love. Just like the Heavenly Father doesn't shrink back from confronting our sin in a loving way, spiritual parents can be used by God to do the same with their own spiritual sons and daughters.

God is looking for spiritual mothers and fathers. Are you one of them? Would you like to be? If this chapter resonates with you, you are probably being called to be a spiritual parent. As I said at the outset, this is a ministry that will find you. God will bring younger people into your life and show both of you that He has divinely arranged this relationship. Let Him open your eyes to see the opportunities all around you.

Do you need a spiritual mother or father in your life? If so, ask God to show you a person you could approach with the request for them to consider such a ministry in your life.

One last word of wisdom: clarify a timeline for the relationship with your spiritual son or daughter. Make a mutual commitment to engage for a period of time, at least six months to a year. This allows time to settle in to the relationship and eventually evaluate the mentorship, providing a smooth way out for either party if needed. Long-term commitments are generally better than short ones. Renew the commitment if God leads you both to continue. Make sure expectations on both sides are clear and mutually agreeable. Be faithful to the commitment you make. Be consistent and dependable. Don't make a commitment you can't keep.

I believe with all my heart that the future of the Kingdom and the church is hopeful and bright because I see so many quality, godly young women and men emerging these days. What an honour it is to play a small part in equipping the next generation!

Let's pray about this right now:

Father, use me to be a spiritual parent. Lead me to the person You have chosen, some-one in whom I can invest my life. Help me to love them with Your love and wisdom.

Deliver me from reluctance, fear, and perfectionism. May my legacy be an empowered generation of Jesus-followers rising up to surpass me in the work of Your Kingdom.

In Jesus's name, amen.

Questions for Reflection

1. Describe a past or current mentoring relationship you've had. What was good about it? What was difficult about it?
2. Of the seven characteristics of a spiritual mother or father, which ones stand out to you the most and why? Which of these qualities do you see in yourself? Which would you like to develop further?
3. Is there someone you know who needs a friend or mentor? How willing are you to offer that ministry to them?
4. Do you need to have a mentor, spiritual mother, or spiritual father in your life? Ask God to lead you to the person of His choosing and talk to them about the possibility of journeying with you.

A Name Better than
Sons and Daughters

Chapter Fifteen

A s this book comes to an end, I want to impart a blessing from our Father to you, dear reader. I have been asking the Lord what He would say to you from His heart, and I want to share what He has given me.

Please ask the Spirit to open your heart to what you're about to hear from your Heavenly Father.

I believe the Heavenly Father wants to give you a new name. He wants to name you according to how He sees you and feels about you. He wants to give you a name better than sons and daughters.

The Lord gave me three passages of scripture that convey this desire of His heart for you.

In the first passage, Isaiah 56:3-5, the Lord speaks a prophetic word to two groups of people that would have every reason to feel marginalized, unimportant, or cast aside—foreigners and eunuchs. Listen to what the Lord says:

> *Let no foreigner who is bound to the Lord say, "The Lord will surely exclude me from his people." And let no eunuch complain, "I am only a dry tree."*
>
> *For this is what the Lord says: "To the eunuchs who keep my Sabbaths, who choose what pleases me and hold fast to my covenant—to them I will give within my temple and its walls a memorial and* a name better than sons and daughters; *I will give them an everlasting name that will endure forever."*
>
> —Isaiah 56:3–5 (emphasis added)

Our Father in heaven wants to give you a name better than sons and daughters, a new name from His heart that will last forever.

I'm grateful that we can even be called sons or daughters of God, but it's astonishing to think that He wants to give us a name *better* than that! As parents carefully and lovingly choose a name for their child, so the Heavenly Father has chosen a name for you. He now wants you to hear it from Him.

In the second passage, Isaiah 62:2–5, the Lord gives this promise of restoration for His chosen people who were either in exile or had recently returned to their desolated homeland:

> *The nations will see your vindication, and all kings your glory;* you will be called by a new name *that the mouth of the Lord will bestow. You will be a crown of splendor in the Lord's hand, a royal diadem in the hand of your God. No longer will they call you Deserted, or name your land Desolate. But you will be called Hephzibah [meaning "my delight is in her"], and your land Beulah [married]; for the Lord will take delight in you, and your land will be married. As a young man marries a young woman, so will your Builder marry you; as a bridegroom rejoices over his bride, so will your God rejoice over you.*
>
> —Isaiah 62:2–5 (emphasis added)

Father, show Your dear child even now Your new name for them. May they have the ears to hear and eyes to see the identity You have declared over them. May they know the destiny You have placed upon their lives. May they embrace the promise of restoration and renewal in their life with You. May they bask in Your love and delight for them.

Then, in the third passage, the Lord gives this promise of a new name to the Philadelphian church in Revelation 3, a church that was small but faithful and steadfast in the face of fierce opposition:

> *The one who is victorious I will make a pillar in the temple of my God. Never again will they leave it. I will write on them the name of my God and the name of the city of my God, the new Jerusalem, which is coming down out of heaven from my God; and* I will also write on them my new name.
>
> —Revelation 3:12 (emphasis added)

My New Name

Let me share the Father's new name for me. I've mentioned it a few times in this book, but you may have missed it.

His name for me is Bobby.

Now, you might be thinking, "But that *is* your name. What's so special about that?" It's incredibly special! You see, my family, friends, teachers, and most adults called me Bobby up until the age of about twelve or thirteen. This changed as I became a young man and people started calling me Bob.

No one calls me Bobby anymore... except for my Heavenly Father.

When the Father calls me Bobby, I feel like a safe, loved, valuable, celebrated child. When He says Bobby, I hear that I am a favoured son, deeply loved and well pleasing to Him. I hear the Father saying this to me over and over again.

I can't begin to tell you how life-giving, affirming, and empowering it is to know this is how the Father sees me and feels about me, reviving a name that I bore in the early seasons of my fatherless life. I can't tell you how much joy and value I feel in my heart when He calls me by my new name.

Dear reader, let the Father rename you. Let Him write His new name upon your heart. This is a very personal experience between you and the Father. Revelation 2:17 says that a person's new name from the Lord is *"known only to the one who receives it."*

Receiving a new name may not make sense to other people, nor is it meant to. It is something intimate and special between you and the Father.

Let His new name for you replace the other names people have labelled you with, or names which have emerged through lies you've believed about yourself. The Father tells you that He has a name for you *better* than son or daughter! What a beautiful mystery. What joy and life!

As I conclude this book, I want to offer a father's prayer of blessing and impartation of the Father's heart upon you:

Father, thank You for being our Father. Thank You for your vast love for each of us as Your children. Thank You for the great love You have lavished upon us that we should be called children of God! (1 John 3:1) Thank You that we belong to You forever and that You love us with an everlasting love.

I bless each reader with the blessing of being a beloved child of the Father. I pray that You will reveal Your new name for each of them—the name that comes from Your heart and tells them how You see them and feel about them. May each of them grow deeper in Your heart of love and become a generation of empowered children who know their Father in greater ways than ever before.

May You increase the new movement of Your Father-heart of love over the whole earth. May we all be participants in multiplying Your love from one person to the next. Through us, Father, spread the genuine, tangible experience of Your love over our families, churches, neighbourhoods, cities, countries, and nations of the world.

I bless all readers with the promise spoken by the Father: "You are my son [or daughter]; today I have become your father. Ask me, and I will make the nations your inheritance, the ends of the earth your possession" *(Psalm 2:7–8). I ask for this in the name of Your Son, the Lord Jesus Christ.*

We love You, Father. We love You. Increase our love for You. Fill our hearts to overflowing with love for You. And when the capacity for love in our hearts is reached, increase our capacity so we can love You even more. I bless all readers with an overflowing cup of the Father's love (Psalm 23:5).

Lord, immerse us all in the deep end of the river of life that flows from Your throne in heaven (Ezekiel 47:1–12). May we move from the shallow end of Your love into the deep end which sweeps us away in its current. May we be well-watered trees on the bank of Your river. And may the fruit of our lives bring healing to many. May many kinds of fish be brought into Your Kingdom, drawn by Your love flowing through us.

In the name of Your Son, Jesus Christ, I bless each reader with an experience of the love of the Father's heart. Fill them now, Father. Transform them now. Heal them now. May they forever be changed by encountering Your heart. May they never be the same again. Thank You for recapturing the hearts of Your people (Ezekiel 14:5). We receive Your promise: "I will give you a new heart and put a new spirit in you; I will remove from you your heart of stone and give you a heart of flesh" *(Ezekiel 36:26).*

I pray all these things in the glorious name of the Father, Son, and Holy Spirit. Amen!

Questions for Reflection

1. How do you understand the concept of receiving a new name from the Lord? How does this concept impact you?

2. Do you know what His name is for you? How willing are you to ask Him to give you His new name? What hesitations might you have?

3. Read again the prayer of blessing and impartation of the Father's heart at the end of this chapter. Personalize it and make it your own. Let it be a platform from which your own prayer grows. Pray it often with faith and longing.

About the Author

Growing up fatherless, Bob has come to experience a profound encounter with his Heavenly Father's love. After a pastoral career of forty years in western Canada, Bob and his wife Audrey continue to actively minister through speaking, mentoring, prayer ministry, counselling, and more. His passion is for people everywhere to encounter the transformative love of the Heavenly Father and find healing and freedom. He holds a Bachelor of Theology from Northwest Baptist Theological College, and a Master of Ministry from Trinity Western University and Seminary. Bob was ordained in 1983.

Bob and Audrey have three adult children and seven grandchildren. They live in Edmonton, Alberta but take every opportunity to escape the city for the Rocky Mountains. This is Bob's first book.

www.bobcarrollauthor.com

BIBLIOGRAPHY

Anderson, Neil T. *Living Free in Christ: The Truth About Who You Are and How Christ Can Meet Your Deepest Needs.* Venture, CA: Regal Books, 1993.

Anderson, Neil T. *Victory Over the Darkness: Realizing the Power of Your Identity in Christ.* Venture, CA: Regal Books, 1990.

Arndt, William, et al. *A Greek-English Lexicon of the New Testament and Other Early Christian Literature.* Chicago IL: University of Chicago Press, 2000.

Balz, Horst R. and Gerhard Schneider. *Exegetical Dictionary of the New Testament.* Grand Rapids, MI: Eerdmans, 2004.

Card, Michael. *Inexpressible: Hesed and the Mystery of God's Loving Kindness.* Downers Grove: InterVarsity Press, 2018.

Carroll, Dave. *The Father's Heart: His Delight, Your Destiny.* Englewood, OH: Village House Press, 2013.

Cook, Jerry and Stanley C. Baldwin. *Love, Acceptance, and Forgiveness: Equipping the Church to Be Truly Christian in a Non-Christian World.* Ventura, CA: Regal Books, 1978.

Dawson, Joy. *Intimate Friendship with God: Through Understanding the Fear of the Lord.* Grand Rapids, MI: Chosen Books, 1986.

Deere, Jack. *Surprised by the Power of the Spirit: Discovering How God Speaks and Heals Today.* Grand Rapids, MI: Zondervan, 1993.

Dickens, Charles. *Great Expectations.* London, UK: Penguin Books, 1996, First published 1860–61.

Eldredge, John. *Fathered By God: Learning What Your Dad Could Never Teach You.* New York, NY: Harper-Collins Publishing, Thomas Nelson, 2009.

Gunter, Sylvia and Arthur Burk. *Blessing Your Spirit With the Blessings of Your Father and the Names of God.* Birmingham, AL: The Father's Business, 2005.

Hart, Archibald D. *Healing Adult Children of Divorce: Taking Care of Unfinished Business So You Can Be Whole Again.* Ann Abor, MI: Servant Publications, Vine Books, 1991.

Horrobin, Peter. *Forgiveness—God's Master Key: Pray the Most Powerful Prayer on Earth.* Lancaster, UK: Sovereign World Ltd., 2008.

Hugget, Joyce. *The Joy of Listening to God: Hearing the Many Ways God Speaks to Us.* Downers Grove, IL: InterVarsity Press, 1986.

Jacobsen, Wayne. *He Loves Me: Learning to Live in the Father's Affection.* Newbury Park, CA: Windblown Media, 2007.

Keller, W. Phillip. *What Is the Father Like? A Devotional Look at How God Cares for His Children.* Minneapolis, MN: Bethany House Publishers, 1996.

Keller, Timothy. *The Prodigal God: Recovering the Heart of the Christian Faith.* New York, NY: Dutton, Penguin Group, 2008.

Kraft, Charles. *I Give You Authority: Practicing the Authority Jesus Gave Us.* Ada MI: Baker Publishing Group, Chosen Books, 2012.

Kreider, Larry. *The Cry for Spiritual Fathers and Mothers.* Ephrata, PA: House to House Publications, 2000.

McClung, Floyd. *Finding Friendship with God.* Seattle, WA: YWAM Publishing, 2005.

McClung, Floyd. *The Father Heart of God: Experiencing the Depths of His Love for You.* Eugene OR: Harvest House Publishers Inc., 2004.

Nouwen, Henri J.M. *The Return of the Prodigal Son: A Story of Homecoming.* New York, NY: Doubleday Publishing, 1994.

Piorek, Ed. *The Father Loves You: An Invitation to Perfect Love.* Cape Town, South Africa: Vineyard International Publishing, 2005.

Reimer, Rob. *Deep Faith: Developing Faith that Releases the Power of God.* Franklin TN: Carpenter's Son Publishing, 2017.

Reimer, Rob. Soul Care: *Seven Transformational Principles for a Healthy Soul.* Franklin TN: Carpenter's Son Publishing, 2016.

Scazzero, Peter. *Emotional Healthy Spirituality.* Grand Rapids, MI: Zondervan, 2017.

Seamands, David A. *Healing for Damaged Emotions.* Colorado Springs, CO: David C. Cook, 2015.

Seamands, David A. *Healing Grace: Let God Free You from the Performance Trap.* Wheaton, IL: Victor Books, Scripture Press Publications, Inc., 1986.

Seamands, David A. *Healing of Memories.* Wheaton, IL: Victor Books, Scripture Press Publications, Inc., 1986.

Smedes, Lewis B. *Forgive and Forget: Healing the Wounds We Don't Deserve.* New York, NY: Harper Collins, 1984.

Symington, Ken. *Loved Like Never Before: Discovering the Father Heart of God.* Lancaster, UK: Sovereign Lord Ltd., 2011.

"We Can Redeem Ourselves": Mother Reunites with Man Who Killed Her Son 26 Years Ago," *CBS.* December 21, 2021 (https://www.cbsnews.com/colorado/news/sharletta-evans-raymond-johnson-casson-evans-deadly-shooting).

Winter, Jack. *The Homecoming: Unconditional Love, Finding Your Place in the Father's Heart.* Seattle, WA: YWAM Publishing, 1999.